TRANSIT COOPERATIVE RESEARCH PROGRAM

NATIONAL COOPERATIVE HIGHWAY RESEARCH PROGRAM

TCRP REPORT 120/NCHRP REPORT 585

Racial and Gender Diversity in State DOTs and Transit Agencies:
A Benchmark Scoping

Hubert H. Humphrey Institute of Public Affairs
UNIVERSITY OF MINNESOTA
Minneapolis, MN

Subject Areas
Planning and Administration • Transportation Law • Public Transit

Research sponsored by the Federal Transit Administration in Cooperation with the Transit Development Corporation and by the American Association of State Highway and Transportation Officials in Cooperation with the Federal Highway Administration

TRANSPORTATION RESEARCH BOARD

WASHINGTON, D.C.
2007
www.TRB.org

TRANSIT COOPERATIVE RESEARCH PROGRAM

The nation's growth and the need to meet mobility, environmental, and energy objectives place demands on public transit systems. Current systems, some of which are old and in need of upgrading, must expand service area, increase service frequency, and improve efficiency to serve these demands. Research is necessary to solve operating problems, to adapt appropriate new technologies from other industries, and to introduce innovations into the transit industry. The Transit Cooperative Research Program (TCRP) serves as one of the principal means by which the transit industry can develop innovative near-term solutions to meet demands placed on it.

The need for TCRP was originally identified in *TRB Special Report 213—Research for Public Transit: New Directions,* published in 1987 and based on a study sponsored by the Urban Mass Transportation Administration—now the Federal Transit Administration (FTA). A report by the American Public Transportation Association (APTA), Transportation 2000, also recognized the need for local, problem-solving research. TCRP, modeled after the longstanding and successful National Cooperative Highway Research Program, undertakes research and other technical activities in response to the needs of transit service providers. The scope of TCRP includes a variety of transit research fields including planning, service configuration, equipment, facilities, operations, human resources, maintenance, policy, and administrative practices.

TCRP was established under FTA sponsorship in July 1992. Proposed by the U.S. Department of Transportation, TCRP was authorized as part of the Intermodal Surface Transportation Efficiency Act of 1991 (ISTEA). On May 13, 1992, a memorandum agreement outlining TCRP operating procedures was executed by the three cooperating organizations: FTA, the National Academies, acting through the Transportation Research Board (TRB); and the Transit Development Corporation, Inc. (TDC), a nonprofit educational and research organization established by APTA. TDC is responsible for forming the independent governing board, designated as the TCRP Oversight and Project Selection (TOPS) Committee.

Research problem statements for TCRP are solicited periodically but may be submitted to TRB by anyone at any time. It is the responsibility of the TOPS Committee to formulate the research program by identifying the highest priority projects. As part of the evaluation, the TOPS Committee defines funding levels and expected products.

Once selected, each project is assigned to an expert panel, appointed by the Transportation Research Board. The panels prepare project statements (requests for proposals), select contractors, and provide technical guidance and counsel throughout the life of the project. The process for developing research problem statements and selecting research agencies has been used by TRB in managing cooperative research programs since 1962. As in other TRB activities, TCRP project panels serve voluntarily without compensation.

Because research cannot have the desired impact if products fail to reach the intended audience, special emphasis is placed on disseminating TCRP results to the intended end users of the research: transit agencies, service providers, and suppliers. TRB provides a series of research reports, syntheses of transit practice, and other supporting material developed by TCRP research. APTA will arrange for workshops, training aids, field visits, and other activities to ensure that results are implemented by urban and rural transit industry practitioners.

The TCRP provides a forum where transit agencies can cooperatively address common operational problems. The TCRP results support and complement other ongoing transit research and training programs.

TCRP REPORT 120

Project J-6 (Task 59)
ISSN 1073-4872
ISBN: 978-0-309-09890-8
Library of Congress Control Number 2007930165

© 2007 Transportation Research Board

COPYRIGHT PERMISSION

Authors herein are responsible for the authenticity of their materials and for obtaining written permissions from publishers or persons who own the copyright to any previously published or copyrighted material used herein.

Cooperative Research Programs (CRP) grants permission to reproduce material in this publication for classroom and not-for-profit purposes. Permission is given with the understanding that none of the material will be used to imply TRB, AASHTO, FAA, FHWA, FMCSA, FTA, or Transit Development Corporation endorsement of a particular product, method, or practice. It is expected that those reproducing the material in this document for educational and not-for-profit uses will give appropriate acknowledgment of the source of any reprinted or reproduced material. For other uses of the material, request permission from CRP.

NOTICE

The project that is the subject of this report was a part of the Transit Cooperative Research Program conducted by the Transportation Research Board with the approval of the Governing Board of the National Research Council. Such approval reflects the Governing Board's judgment that the project concerned is appropriate with respect to both the purposes and resources of the National Research Council.

The members of the technical advisory panel selected to monitor this project and to review this report were chosen for recognized scholarly competence and with due consideration for the balance of disciplines appropriate to the project. The opinions and conclusions expressed or implied are those of the research agency that performed the research, and while they have been accepted as appropriate by the technical panel, they are not necessarily those of the Transportation Research Board, the National Research Council, the Transit Development Corporation, or the Federal Transit Administration of the U.S. Department of Transportation.

Each report is reviewed and accepted for publication by the technical panel according to procedures established and monitored by the Transportation Research Board Executive Committee and the Governing Board of the National Research Council.

The Transportation Research Board of the National Academies, the National Research Council, the Transit Development Corporation, and the Federal Transit Administration (sponsor of the Transit Cooperative Research Program) do not endorse products or manufacturers. Trade or manufacturers' names appear herein solely because they are considered essential to the clarity and completeness of the project reporting.

Published reports of the

TRANSIT COOPERATIVE RESEARCH PROGRAM

are available from:

Transportation Research Board
Business Office
500 Fifth Street, NW
Washington, DC 20001

and can be ordered through the Internet at
http://www.national-academies.org/trb/bookstore

Printed in the United States of America

NATIONAL COOPERATIVE HIGHWAY RESEARCH PROGRAM

Systematic, well-designed research provides the most effective approach to the solution of many problems facing highway administrators and engineers. Often, highway problems are of local interest and can best be studied by highway departments individually or in cooperation with their state universities and others. However, the accelerating growth of highway transportation develops increasingly complex problems of wide interest to highway authorities. These problems are best studied through a coordinated program of cooperative research.

In recognition of these needs, the highway administrators of the American Association of State Highway and Transportation Officials initiated in 1962 an objective national highway research program employing modern scientific techniques. This program is supported on a continuing basis by funds from participating member states of the Association and it receives the full cooperation and support of the Federal Highway Administration, United States Department of Transportation.

The Transportation Research Board of the National Academies was requested by the Association to administer the research program because of the Board's recognized objectivity and understanding of modern research practices. The Board is uniquely suited for this purpose as it maintains an extensive committee structure from which authorities on any highway transportation subject may be drawn; it possesses avenues of communications and cooperation with federal, state and local governmental agencies, universities, and industry; its relationship to the National Research Council is an insurance of objectivity; it maintains a full-time research correlation staff of specialists in highway transportation matters to bring the findings of research directly to those who are in a position to use them.

The program is developed on the basis of research needs identified by chief administrators of the highway and transportation departments and by committees of AASHTO. Each year, specific areas of research needs to be included in the program are proposed to the National Research Council and the Board by the American Association of State Highway and Transportation Officials. Research projects to fulfill these needs are defined by the Board, and qualified research agencies are selected from those that have submitted proposals. Administration and surveillance of research contracts are the responsibilities of the National Research Council and the Transportation Research Board.

The needs for highway research are many, and the National Cooperative Highway Research Program can make significant contributions to the solution of highway transportation problems of mutual concern to many responsible groups. The program, however, is intended to complement rather than to substitute for or duplicate other highway research programs.

NCHRP REPORT 585

Project 20-24 (47)
ISSN 0077-5614
ISBN: 978-0-309-09890-8
Library of Congress Control Number 2007930165

© 2007 Transportation Research Board

COPYRIGHT PERMISSION

Authors herein are responsible for the authenticity of their materials and for obtaining written permissions from publishers or persons who own the copyright to any previously published or copyrighted material used herein.

Cooperative Research Programs (CRP) grants permission to reproduce material in this publication for classroom and not-for-profit purposes. Permission is given with the understanding that none of the material will be used to imply TRB, AASHTO, FAA, FHWA, FMCSA, FTA, or Transit Development Corporation endorsement of a particular product, method, or practice. It is expected that those reproducing the material in this document for educational and not-for-profit uses will give appropriate acknowledgment of the source of any reprinted or reproduced material. For other uses of the material, request permission from CRP.

NOTICE

The project that is the subject of this report was a part of the National Cooperative Highway Research Program conducted by the Transportation Research Board with the approval of the Governing Board of the National Research Council. Such approval reflects the Governing Board's judgment that the program concerned is of national importance and appropriate with respect to both the purposes and resources of the National Research Council.

The members of the technical committee selected to monitor this project and to review this report were chosen for recognized scholarly competence and with due consideration for the balance of disciplines appropriate to the project. The opinions and conclusions expressed or implied are those of the research agency that performed the research, and, while they have been accepted as appropriate by the technical committee, they are not necessarily those of the Transportation Research Board, the National Research Council, the American Association of State Highway and Transportation Officials, or the Federal Highway Administration, U.S. Department of Transportation.

Each report is reviewed and accepted for publication by the technical committee according to procedures established and monitored by the Transportation Research Board Executive Committee and the Governing Board of the National Research Council.

The Transportation Research Board of the National Academies, the National Research Council, the Federal Highway Administration, the American Association of State Highway and Transportation Officials, and the individual states participating in the National Cooperative Highway Research Program do not endorse products or manufacturers. Trade or manufacturers' names appear herein solely because they are considered essential to the object of this report.

Published reports of the

NATIONAL COOPERATIVE HIGHWAY RESEARCH PROGRAM

are available from:

Transportation Research Board
Business Office
500 Fifth Street, NW
Washington, DC 20001

and can be ordered through the Internet at:

http://www.national-academies.org/trb/bookstore

Printed in the United States of America

COOPERATIVE RESEARCH PROGRAMS

CRP STAFF FOR TCRP REPORT 120/NCHRP REPORT 585

Christopher W. Jenks, *Director, Cooperative Research Programs*
Crawford F. Jencks, *Deputy Director, Cooperative Research Programs*
Gwen Chisholm-Smith, *Senior Program Officer*
Eileen P. Delaney, *Director of Publications*

TCRP PROJECT J-06, TASK 59/NCHRP PROJECT 20-24(47) PANEL
Field of Special Projects

Anne P. Canby, *Surface Transportation Policy Project, Washington, DC* (Chair)
Carlos Arce, *NuStats Partners, LP, Austin TX*
Jeff Boothe, *Holland & Knight LLP, Washington, DC*
Julie Cunningham, *COMTO, Washington, DC*
Mary J. Davis, *McGlothin Davis Inc., Denver, CO*
Thomas M. Downs, *ENO Transportation Foundation, Inc., Washington, DC*
Gloria J. Jeff, *Los Angeles DOT*
Z. Wayne Johnson, *Sacramento Regional Transit District*
Maria Krysan, *University of Illinois–Chicago*
Stephanie L. Pinson, *Gilbert Tweed Associates, Inc., New York, NY*
Janette Sadik-Khan, *New York City Department of Transportation, NY*
Tate Jackson, *AASHTO Liaison*
Pamela Boswell, *APTA Liaison*
Suzanne Schneider, *TRB Liaison*

AUTHOR ACKNOWLEDGMENTS

Principal Investigator: Samuel L. Myers, Jr., Roy Wilkins Center for Human Relations and Social Justice
Co-Authors: Lawrencina Mason Oramalu, Irma Arteaga, Lan Pham
Research Team: Stephannie Lewis, Abigail Read, Todd Stump
Wilkins Center Staff: Mary Lou Middleton
Project Consultant: Kevin Krizek
Project Manager: James Gee, CompuCon, Alexandria, VA
Editor: Julia Blount

THE NATIONAL ACADEMIES
Advisers to the Nation on Science, Engineering, and Medicine

The **National Academy of Sciences** is a private, nonprofit, self-perpetuating society of distinguished scholars engaged in scientific and engineering research, dedicated to the furtherance of science and technology and to their use for the general welfare. On the authority of the charter granted to it by the Congress in 1863, the Academy has a mandate that requires it to advise the federal government on scientific and technical matters. Dr. Ralph J. Cicerone is president of the National Academy of Sciences.

The **National Academy of Engineering** was established in 1964, under the charter of the National Academy of Sciences, as a parallel organization of outstanding engineers. It is autonomous in its administration and in the selection of its members, sharing with the National Academy of Sciences the responsibility for advising the federal government. The National Academy of Engineering also sponsors engineering programs aimed at meeting national needs, encourages education and research, and recognizes the superior achievements of engineers. Dr. Charles M. Vest is president of the National Academy of Engineering.

The **Institute of Medicine** was established in 1970 by the National Academy of Sciences to secure the services of eminent members of appropriate professions in the examination of policy matters pertaining to the health of the public. The Institute acts under the responsibility given to the National Academy of Sciences by its congressional charter to be an adviser to the federal government and, on its own initiative, to identify issues of medical care, research, and education. Dr. Harvey V. Fineberg is president of the Institute of Medicine.

The **National Research Council** was organized by the National Academy of Sciences in 1916 to associate the broad community of science and technology with the Academy's purposes of furthering knowledge and advising the federal government. Functioning in accordance with general policies determined by the Academy, the Council has become the principal operating agency of both the National Academy of Sciences and the National Academy of Engineering in providing services to the government, the public, and the scientific and engineering communities. The Council is administered jointly by both the Academies and the Institute of Medicine. Dr. Ralph J. Cicerone and Dr. Charles M. Vest are chair and vice chair, respectively, of the National Research Council.

The **Transportation Research Board** is a division of the National Research Council, which serves the National Academy of Sciences and the National Academy of Engineering. The Board's mission is to promote innovation and progress in transportation through research. In an objective and interdisciplinary setting, the Board facilitates the sharing of information on transportation practice and policy by researchers and practitioners; stimulates research and offers research management services that promote technical excellence; provides expert advice on transportation policy and programs; and disseminates research results broadly and encourages their implementation. The Board's varied activities annually engage more than 5,000 engineers, scientists, and other transportation researchers and practitioners from the public and private sectors and academia, all of whom contribute their expertise in the public interest. The program is supported by state transportation departments, federal agencies including the component administrations of the U.S. Department of Transportation, and other organizations and individuals interested in the development of transportation. **www.TRB.org**

www.national-academies.org

FOREWORD

By Gwen Chisholm-Smith
Staff Officer
Transportation Research Board

TCRP Report 120/NCHRP Report 585: Racial and Gender Diversity in State DOTs and Transit Agencies documents and analyzes racial and gender diversity in state departments of transportation (state DOTs) and transit agencies for purposes of establishing a baseline that reflects the current status of racial and gender diversity in state DOTs and transit agencies based on existing data. This report will be useful to Chief Administrative Officers of state DOTs, Chief Executive Officers of transit agencies, state DOT officials, transit officials, and other transportation professionals interested in workforce development.

The United States of America is a diverse nation. According to the 2000 U.S. Census, minorities constitute about 30% of the population. Between 2002 and 2012, the number of minorities in the U.S. labor force is projected to increase faster than the number of whites (*Occupational Outlook Quarterly*, p. 28, Bureau of Labor Statistics, Summer 2004). Moreover, women's share of the labor force will also continue to increase, reaching 47.5% by 2012 (*Minority Labor Review* February 2004).

The impact of these trends on the employment composition of some U.S. industries remains largely unknown. Despite the availability of many reports on workforce challenges facing the U.S. transportation industry, the representational data available on its employees by gender and race are limited. Such data are needed by state DOTs and transit agencies to assess the current diversity of their workforce; to establish a benchmark against which to measure and track efforts to recruit, promote, and retain a diverse workforce; and to identify successful practices being applied throughout the industry.

The objectives of this project were to: (1) identify sources of existing data on the race and gender of employees of state DOTs, transit agencies, and contract employees of public transit agencies; (2) assess the quality of the data in terms of their comprehensiveness, validity, and reliability; (3) identify gaps discovered in the existing data and determine what additional data need to be collected in order to establish a credible benchmark; and (4) establish a baseline reflecting the current status of racial and gender diversity in state DOTs and transit agencies based on existing data.

This report was prepared by Dr. Samuel Myers, Jr. and Lawrencina Mason Oramalu, of University of Minnesota, Roy Wilkins Center for Human Relations and Social Justice. The research for this report consisted of a review of pertinent literature related to promoting, recruiting, and retaining a diverse workforce. Also, the research team collected information from the equal employment opportunity (EEO) files provided by the Federal Transit Administration and the Federal Highway Administration, and the research team developed and administered a web survey of state DOTs.

The research revealed that the EEO data submitted on existing employees by transit agencies and state DOTs was incomplete and not comprehensive, making it challenging to establish a credible benchmark. This report provides a conceptual framework that addresses the type of data that is needed to establish a credible benchmark.

CONTENTS

- **1** Summary
- **3 Chapter 1** Background
  - 3 Problem Statement and Research Objective
  - 3 Organization
  - 3 Legislative History and Intent
- **7 Chapter 2** Research Approach
  - 7 Review of the Available Literature
  - 7 Review of Existing Transportation Data
  - 7 Review of Available Datasets
  - 7 Administration and Analysis of Web Survey
  - 8 Conceptual Framework
- **10 Chapter 3** Findings and Applications
  - 10 State Departments of Transportation
  - 20 Transit Agencies
- **26 Chapter 4** Conclusions and Recommendations
  - 26 Conclusions
  - 26 Recommendations
  - 28 Suggestions for Further Research
- **29** References
- **30 Appendix A**   Affirmative Action Timeline
- **33 Appendix B**   Literature Review
- **37 Appendix C**   Bibliography
- **39 Appendix D**   Survey Findings
- **44 Appendix E**   Best Practices
- **51 Appendix F**   Acronyms and Abbreviations

SUMMARY

Racial and Gender Diversity in State DOTs and Transit Agencies: A Benchmark Scoping

The purpose of this project was to analyze the current level of racial and gender diversity in state departments of transportation (SDOTs) and transit agencies, with the goal of establishing a baseline and benchmarks for employment diversity.

This benchmark scoping project exemplifies the transportation industry's commitment to expanding opportunities for women and minorities. The industry has a long history of promoting diversity, primarily through external programs such as the disadvantaged business enterprise (DBE) program, and it now seeks to strengthen its internal diversity programs by developing and monitoring a benchmark for achieving racial and gender diversity in SDOTs and transit agencies.

This project had four key objectives:

1. Identify sources of existing data on the race and gender of employees of SDOTs and transit agencies (including contract employees of public transit agencies).
2. Assess the quality of the data in terms of comprehensiveness, validity, and reliability.
3. Identify gaps in the existing data and determine what additional data need to be collected to establish a credible benchmark.
4. Establish a baseline reflecting the current status of racial and gender diversity in SDOTs and transit agencies.

To accomplish these four objectives, the research team reviewed the equal employment opportunity (EEO) files provided by the Federal Highway Administration and the Federal Transit Administration, conducted a review of the available literature; and developed and administered a web survey of SDOTs.

Findings

Existing Data

Data on the race and gender of current employees of SDOTs and transit agencies are reported on the EEO-4 form, which state and local government agencies complete as a part of their EEO programs. Agencies report the number of women and minorities employed within the following EEO categories: officials and administrators, professionals, technicians, protective service workers, administrative support, skilled craft workers, and service maintenance (an eighth category—paraprofessionals—is not included in this analysis as comparison data are not available from the Census Bureau).

SDOTs also submit EEO data on FHWA-1392, the Federal-Aid Highway Construction Summary of Employment Data form, which reflects the total employment on Federal-Aid Highway Program projects.

Quality of the Data

Overall, the existing data on employees of SDOTs and transit agencies is not comprehensive. For the data to be considered comprehensive, SDOTs need to complete and submit an affirmative action plan and an EEO-4 report, as well as a utilization and availability analysis in their EEO programs. The research team received and reviewed EEO-4 forms for more than 90% of SDOTs and for more than 60% of the largest transit agencies.

Gaps in the Data

There were several gaps between the existing data and the data that should be collected to establish a credible benchmark. The research team developed a conceptual framework, the four Cs, which addresses the type of data that is needed to establish a credible benchmark.

- If an agency is *compliant*,
- If an agency's data are *consistent*,
- If an agency's data are *comprehensive*, and
- If the agency is *confident* in the data it is reporting,
- Then the data are more likely to be *valid and reliable*.

CHAPTER 1

Background

According to the *Occupational Outlook Quarterly*, "Between 2002 and 2012, the number of minorities in the U.S. labor force is projected to increase faster than the number of whites" (*1*). The number of women in the workforce is also projected to increase, with women expected to account for 47.5% of the workforce by 2012 (*2*). Both the public and private transportation sectors will be influenced by these changing demographics.

The transportation industry makes up a significant portion of the total civilian workforce, accounting for one in 10 employees. According to *The Workforce Challenge: Recruiting, Training, and Retaining Qualified Workers for Transportation and Transit Agencies*, "Total transportation employment in the United States is more than 14.7 million, about 11 percent of the civilian workforce" (*3*). State departments of transportation (SDOTs) and transit agencies are competing not only with each other, but also with the private sector, to recruit and retain qualified employees from among nearly 15 million available workers. Federal and state governments espouse equal employment opportunities, and SDOTs and transit agencies should strive to recruit and retain not only a qualified workforce, but also a diverse workforce. This project is designed to assist SDOTs and transit agencies in achieving that goal.

Problem Statement and Research Objective

The project was designed to identify, analyze, and assess the quality of employment data for SDOTs and transit agencies. It had the following four objectives:

1. Identify sources of existing data on the race and gender of employees of SDOTs and transit agencies (including contract employees of public transit agencies).
2. Assess the quality of the data in terms of comprehensiveness, validity, and reliability.
3. Identify gaps in the existing data and determine what additional data need to be collected to establish a credible benchmark.
4. Establish a baseline reflecting the current status of racial and gender diversity in SDOTs and transit agencies.

Organization

This report is divided into four chapters, followed by several appendixes. The first chapter presents an overview of the project, including the project's background, the report's organization, the methodology employed, and the legislative history of affirmative action.

The second chapter outlines the conceptual framework that the research team developed as a result of its analyses. It discusses how four key concepts—compliance, consistency, comprehensiveness, and confidence—are essential to a successful diversity or affirmative action program.

The third chapter presents the results of the team's analysis of utilization and disproportionality rates for SDOTs and transit agencies. In the fourth chapter, the team outlines it recommendations for achieving a diverse workforce.

Several important resources are included in the Appendixes:

- Appendix A—Affirmative Action Timeline
- Appendix B—Literature Review
- Appendix C—Bibliography
- Appendix D—Survey Findings
- Appendix E—Best Practices
- Appendix F—Acronyms and Abbreviations

Legislative History and Intent

Achieving a diverse workforce is part of a federal mandate that dates back to the 1960s. During the civil rights movement of the 1960s, the federal government made equal employment opportunity (EEO) the law of the land (*4*). The executive branch issued executive orders, Congress passed legislation, and agencies promulgated regulations that prohibited discrimination and required federal contractors to develop affirmative action plans. These executive orders, laws, and regulations were designed to expand employment opportunities for women and minorities, both of whom had previously been subject to institutional discrimination.

EEO Programs in the United States

President John F. Kennedy's Executive Order 10925 of 1961 prohibited federal government contractors from discriminating on the basis of race, instructing employers "to ensure that applicants are employed, and that employees are treated during employment, without regard to their race, creed, color, or national origin." This executive order (subsequently superseded by Executive Order 11246 of 1965) was the first of several key events in the history of civil rights that have shaped the affirmative action discourse and given employers guidance on how to develop EEO programs. Those events include the passage of Title VI of the Civil Rights Act of 1964, which prohibits discrimination under any program that receives federal financial assistance (5) and Title VII of the Civil Rights Act, which prohibits employment discrimination based on race, sex, color, religion, or national origin (6).

Title VII was enacted in an effort to expand employment opportunities for groups underrepresented in the workforce, specifically women and minorities.

> It shall be an unlawful employment practice for an employer to fail or refuse to hire or to discharge any individual, or otherwise to discriminate against any individual with respect to his compensation, terms, conditions, or privileges of employment, because of such individual's race, color, religion, sex, or national origin; or to limit, segregate, or classify his employees or applicants for employment in a way which would deprive or tend to deprive any individual of employment opportunities or otherwise adversely affect his status as an employee, because of such individual's race, color, religion, sex or national origin. (6)

During the congressional debate leading to passage of the Civil Rights Act, the Senate discussed "the plight of the Negro in our economy" and the need for the government to intervene (7). Prior to the enactment of Title VII, Blacks were relegated to unskilled and semi-skilled jobs, and the numbers of those jobs were declining due to automation. As a result, employment opportunities for Blacks had worsened. "In 1947 the nonwhite unemployment rate was only 64 percent higher than the white rate; in 1962 it was 124 percent higher" (8).

Following the passage of Title VII, employers sought guidance on how to develop EEO programs in compliance with the law. In response, in 1976 the Department of Labor, Equal Employment Opportunity Commission (EEOC), Civil Service Commission, Attorney General's Office, and Commission on Civil Rights (which together constituted the Equal Employment Opportunity Coordinating Council) formulated a policy statement on affirmative action. This statement was designed to provide guidance to government agencies on the role of affirmative action in EEO programs.

> Equal employment opportunity is the law of the land. In the public sector of our society this means that all persons, regardless of race, color, religion, sex, or national origin shall have equal access to positions in the public service limited only by their ability to do the job. There is ample evidence in all sectors of our society that such equal access frequently has been denied to members of certain groups because of their sex, racial, or ethnic characteristics. (4)

In this policy statement, the Equal Employment Opportunity Coordinating Council "urges all State and local governments to develop and implement results oriented affirmative action plans."

Affirmative action can take the form of race-neutral or race-conscious measures, but if race-conscious measures are used, agencies may subject themselves to a charge of reverse discrimination. According to the EEOC, in enacting Title VII, "Congress did not intend to expose those who comply with the Act to charges that they are violating the very statute they are seeking to implement. Such a result would immobilize or reduce the efforts of many who would otherwise take action to improve the opportunities of minorities and women without litigation, thus frustrating the Congressional intent to encourage voluntary action and increasing the prospect of Title VII litigation" (9).

Over the past 10 years, there have been several legal challenges to affirmative action policies, not only in employment, but also in education and in government contracting. These legal challenges have affected the political atmosphere and fueled the debate on whether affirmative action policies are appropriate under Title VII.

To understand the current state of affirmative action in terms of what types of measures are appropriate under Title VII, it is helpful to review the legal history of affirmative action. A thorough history is discussed in the report, *Affirmative Action Revisited: A Legal History and Prospectus* (10), as well as outlined on several websites (including www.eeoc.gov and www.detroitnaacp.org). A timeline highlighting key events in the history of affirmative action is provided in Appendix A. In short, the history reveals that employers are to make "good faith efforts" to achieve a diverse workforce, and their race-conscious goals are supposed to be "narrowly tailored," justified by a "compelling interest," and should not "unnecessarily trammel" the rights of nonminorities.

EEO Regulations in the Department of Transportation

SDOTs and transit agencies must adhere not only to federal executive orders, state and federal legislation, and case law, but also to regulations that have been promulgated by the U.S. Department of Transportation (USDOT). Within USDOT, SDOTs fall under the purview of the Federal Highway Administration (FHWA), and transit agencies fall under the purview of the Federal Transit Administration (FTA). Both of these agencies have developed guidelines on the implementation of EEO programs at state and local transportation agencies.

Although SDOTs and transit agencies report to two different federal authorities, all transportation agencies are governed by two regulations: Nondiscrimination in Federally Assisted Programs of the Department of Transportation (*11*), which addresses employment within transportation agencies, and Participation by Disadvantaged Business Enterprises in Department of Transportation Financial Assistance Programs (*12*), which deals with government contracts with external organizations.

The purpose of the Nondiscrimination in Federally Assisted Programs of the Department of Transportation "is to effectuate the provisions of title VI of the Civil Rights Act of 1964 . . . to the end that no person in the United States shall, on the grounds of race, color, or national origin, be excluded from participation in, be denied the benefits of, or be otherwise subjected to discrimination under any program or activity receiving Federal financial assistance from the Department of Transportation." The regulation goes on to state:

> Where a primary objective of a program of Federal financial assistance . . . is to provide employment, a recipient or other party . . . shall not . . . subject a person to discrimination on the ground of race, color, or national origin in its employment practices under such program (including recruitment advertising, hiring, firing, upgrading, promotion, demotion, transfer, layoff, termination, rates of pay or other forms of compensation or benefits, selection for training or apprenticeship, use of facilities, and treatment of employees). Such recipient shall take affirmative action to insure that applicants are employed, and employees are treated during employment, without regard to their race, color, or national origin.

Although the regulations clearly authorize transportation agencies to take affirmative steps in the area of employment, transportation agencies that have taken such steps have been challenged.

In 1973, the U.S. Supreme Court upheld a county transit agency's voluntary affirmative action plan in *Johnson v. Transportation Agency*, in which the Transportation Agency of Santa Clara County, California, was using gender as a factor in determining promotions within traditionally segregated job classifications. "Women were significantly underrepresented in the county's labor force as a whole and in five of seven job categories, including skilled crafts where all 238 employees were men. The plan's long range goal was proportional representation" (480 U.S. 616, 1987). The court approved the county's plan because it satisfied the "manifest imbalance" requirement established in *United Steelworkers v. Weber* (443 U.S. 193, 1979). In *Weber*, the court upheld a voluntary affirmative action plan that set aside slots for minorities in an effort "to increase the percentage of blacks in skilled craft positions from 2% to the level of their overall participation in the area workforce, or 39%" (*10*). The Supreme Court ruled in favor of the union, arguing that "'racial preferences" in the program were a lawful means to combat 'manifest racial imbalance' in craft positions resulting from "old patterns of racial segregation and hierarchy"'(*13*).

Transportation agencies are authorized to use affirmative action not only in employment practices, but also in government contracting and procurement practices. Agencies receiving federal transportation funds are required to have a disadvantaged business enterprise (DBE) program. According to USDOT, the DBE program is intended "to remedy past and current discrimination against disadvantaged business enterprises, ensure a 'level playing field' in which DBEs can compete fairly for DOT-assisted contracts, improve the flexibility and efficiency of the DBE program, and reduce burdens on small businesses" (www.dotcr.ost.dot.gov/asp/dbe.asp).

After several amendments to the original 1983 regulation and following the Supreme Court's ruling in *Adarand* (513 U.S. 1012, 1994), USDOT issued a final rule in 1999, which was designed to give agencies clear instructions on how to develop narrowly tailored DBE goal programs, in compliance with the legal standard articulated in *Adarand*. The rule was later revised in 2003 to provide grantees with additional guidance on how to develop legally defensible hiring goals.

DBE programs have been challenged by those who argue that the programs are unconstitutional. The most recent challenge came in *Western States Paving Co. v. United States & Washington State Department of Transportation* (407 F. 3d 983, 9th Cir., 2005). In 2006, FTA issued a notice of policy implementation in the *Federal Register* to help grantees understand the impact this decision might have on their DBE programs. Although the Court ruled that Washington DOT had unconstitutionally applied the DBE regulation, the notice also stressed that the Court "affirmed that Congress had determined that there was a compelling need for the DBE program and the Part 26 was narrowly tailored" (*14*).

Although this decision addresses affirmative action programs in government contracting, the underlying issues can be applied to affirmative action in employment. For example, "the court said that race conscious elements of a national program, to be narrowly tailored as applied, must be limited to those parts of the country where its race-based measures are demonstrably needed." Similarly, for an affirmative action or diversity program in employment to be narrowly tailored, it must be limited to the part of the country where there is a need, and there must be evidence of discrimination; the remedy must be limited to the particular group that experienced the discrimination. Evidence of discrimination should be based on a statistical analysis, not just anecdotal reports.

Affirmative action, if properly designed and applied, is thus still allowed under both Title VII of the Civil Rights Act and USDOT's regulations regarding nondiscrimination in federally assisted programs. The Policy Statement on Affirmative Action says that affirmative action plans may include numerical goals and timetables (not quotas) and career advancement training programs (4). The goals and timetables should be based on a statistical analysis of the employer's workforce and of the workers in the relevant job market.

EEO Reporting Requirements

EEOC, the agency charged with primary enforcement authority, has developed reporting requirements for public and private employers. Private-sector employers with more than 100 employees, as well as those employers that have federal government contracts worth $50,000 or more and that have 50 or more employees, must complete the Employer Information Report (EEO-1). This report must be submitted annually to EEOC; if the employer receives federal funds, a copy must also be submitted to the Office of Federal Contract Compliance Programs (OFCCP). EEOC uses this information to support civil rights enforcement and to analyze employment patterns, such as the representation of female and minority workers in companies, industries, or regions (www.eeoc.gov/stats/jobpat/e1instruct.html).

Since 1973, state and local governments with 100 or more employees have been required to submit a State and Local Government Report (EEO-4); the report provides information on the number of women and minorities in eight job categories.

The EEO-4 reports submitted to FHWA by SDOTs and to FTA by transit agencies were analyzed for this project, with the intent of developing a diversity baseline. Because SDOTs and transit agencies have different missions, goals, organizational structures, and reporting requirements, the analyses are presented separately in this report.

CHAPTER 2

Research Approach

Methods to collect and analyze information for this project included

- A review of the available literature,
- A review of existing transportation data and datasets,
- The administration and analysis of a web survey, and
- An analysis of utilization and availability rates.

Review of the Available Literature

A literature search was conducted using traditional academic search engines. In addition, a targeted search was conducted using TRB's Transportation Research Information Services (TRIS). A summary of the literature review is provided in Appendix B, and a list of references consulted appears in Appendix C.

Review of Existing Transportation Data

The research team reviewed the most recent affirmative action plans and EEO forms submitted by the 52 SDOTs (from each of the 50 states plus Washington, D.C., and Puerto Rico) and the 50 largest transit agencies (which account for 80% of all transit employees). The forms, which were provided by FHWA and FTA, were reviewed for comprehensiveness, validity, and consistency in how the agencies report their employment data.

A preliminary review of SDOT data led to the conclusion that only a limited analysis could be performed because the data were available only in hard copy format and because of variances in *what* information was reported and *how* the information was reported.

The research team reviewed the reporting requirements for SDOTs (*16*) and those for transit agencies (*15*). The team also interviewed FHWA and FTA staff.

The research team learned that there is no central location for electronically storing EEO forms submitted by SDOTs or transit agencies. Because the information is only available in hard copy, the team created a template that would allow them to readily inventory the key information included in the various reports. In addition, a database was created to track reported utilization and availability rates, as well as disproportionality rates (if a disproportionality rate was not provided, the research team calculated it).

Review of Available Datasets

Employment data obtained from the U.S. Census Bureau's Summary File 4 (SF-4) were used to check the validity of the availability rates reported by the agencies. Employment counts were collected for total employees, total minorities, Blacks (non-Hispanic), Hispanics or Latinos, American Indians, Asians, and Whites (non-Hispanic); the counts were further broken down by gender and by occupational group.

State and county demographic information was retrieved from the Census Bureau's website (www.quickfacts.census.gov/qfd/) to determine if any of the demographic information, such as unemployment rate, poverty rate, population, or density, could explain the actual or perceived disparity in the SDOTs' utilization and availability of women and minorities.

Administration and Analysis of Web Survey

The research team prepared a web survey that would be administered to all 52 SDOTs, with the goal of measuring the SDOTs' level of confidence in the employment data they collect and submit.

The web survey was based on the framework discussed in John Milam's 1996 report, *National Study of Faculty Availability and Utilization*, in which the author outlines several research questions that should be addressed during an availability and utilization analysis (highered.org/docs/milam-facultyavailability.pdf). Although Milam's article focuses on faculty hiring, the research questions are equally applicable to this project. Milam poses the following research questions:

- What is the status of affirmative action plans for faculty hiring?
- Are there principles and rules to guide affirmative action/EEO officers in preparing these plans?
- Are consistent, reliable data available for measuring how well institutions are doing in attracting a diverse faculty?
- How are these data collected, analyzed, disseminated, and used internally?

Milam also lists some specific questions that should be answered in an availability and utilization report:

- Do institutions complete an affirmative action plan with availability data?
- How often are these plans produced?
- Are availability and utilization analyses reported?
- What sources are used for gathering faculty availability data?
- Who calculates the availability data?
- How are the data calculated?
- How are availability and utilization data broken out?
- Are numerical goals and/or availability data shared with search committees?
- Are the provost and/or academic deans involved in determining availability data?

Those questions, modified for SDOT purposes, were used to develop the web survey. The survey instrument was divided into three main categories: EEO reporting, availability and utilization information, and information about the respondent.

Five SDOTs were selected to pretest the survey (five of the nine Census regions were randomly selected, and then one state was randomly selected in each of those five regions). This allowed the research team to obtain suggestions and comments from people who work directly in human resource departments in SDOTs, who deal with racial and gender diversity issues, and who work in different regions of the country. This last characteristic was fundamental to the study because different regions may have different cultural approaches to these issues. Four of the five SDOTs asked to participate in the pretest completed the survey.

After the team reviewed the results of the pretest, the survey was modified and then administered to the remaining 47 SDOTs. E-mails were sent to the SDOT civil rights directors, asking them for help in gaining insight into the availability and utilization of women and minorities in their agencies. This e-mail included a cover letter with a link to the website containing the survey, as well as a consent statement. A reminder email was sent to the directors one week later.

Twenty-nine SDOTs responded to the survey.

The main findings from the survey are summarized in Appendix D.

Conceptual Framework

After reviewing and analyzing the EEO files from the SDOTs and transit agencies, several issues emerged related to compliance, consistency, comprehensiveness, and confidence (the four Cs).

First, some agencies did not submit the proper EEO documentation.

Second, agencies do not report their EEO information in a consistent manner.

Third, the level of comprehensiveness of the reports differ, with significant variations in content and thoroughness.

Fourth, some agencies expressed a lack of confidence in their data, unsure whether the data were valid and reliable.

To determine if the SDOT and transit agency data that it was reviewing were valid and reliable, the research team developed a conceptual framework for evaluation, based on the key issues and concerns that emerged while reviewing the data (see Table 1).

If an agency is *compliant* in its reporting of data, if an agency's data are *consistent* with that reported by other agencies, if an agency's data are *comprehensive* in content and thoroughness, and if the agency is *confident* of the quality of the data, then the data are likely to be valid and reliable.

To help determine how well an agency's data fares under this four-pronged framework, the research team created a template for storing the information provided in SDOT and transit agency reports. The template was based on the following questions:

- Was an EEO-4 form submitted?
- What was the date of the EEO-4 form?
- If no EEO-4 form was submitted, were the EEO-4 numbers provided in the text of the report?
- Was an FHWA-1392 (Federal Aid Highway Construction: Summary of Employment Data) form submitted?
- What was the date of the Form 1392?
- Was an overall utilization rate provided?
- Was a utilization rate provided for each race/ethnic group?
- Were utilization rates provided by gender?
- Were utilization rates cross-referenced for race and gender?
- Was an overall availability rate provided?
- Was an availability rate provided by race/ethnic group?
- Was an availability rate provided by gender?
- Was availability cross-referenced for race and gender?
- What was the date of the availability data?
- Did the agency report a disparity ratio or underutilization?
- What minority/ethnic categories were used?

Table 1. Conceptual Framework for Evaluating if Data Are Valid and Reliable.

Compliance	Consistency	Comprehensiveness	Certainty
Agency submits an affirmative action plan.	Agencies provide employment counts based on the same Census data.	Agency provides both utilization and availability counts.	Agency is certain of the accuracy of the EEO information provided.
Agency submits an EEO-4 form.	Agencies' employment counts use the same racial/ethnic classifications.	Agency develops targeted goals for women and minorities.	
Agency provides employment counts for women and minorities.			
Agency provides disaggregated employment counts for women and minorities.	Agencies' employment counts are broken down by EEO-4 classifications.		

Information gleaned from the web survey and data collected from the Census Bureau were used to run numerous statistical tests designed to answer the following questions:

- What factors might explain an agency's failure to comply with the regulations regarding EEO reporting?
- What are some of the characteristics of compliant and noncompliant agencies?
- Why did some agencies report their incumbency/utilization data in a different way?
- Why did some agencies submit information on availability, while others did not?
- Are the agencies confident in the data they submitted? Should the agencies be confident in the data they submitted?
- Was there a difference between the availability reported for an agency and the availability rate calculated using the Census data?
- Did the agencies compare their utilization and availability rates?
- Did the agencies find any underrepresentation or disproportionality?
- Did the research team find any underrepresentation or disproportionality using independent calculations?
- What occupations and racial/gender groups account for the most disproportionality?

The research team conducted a series of regression analyses to better understand the factors that explain compliance. Demographic factors seemingly had little, if any, effect on which SDOTs or transit agencies fully complied with requirements for filing EEO-4 forms; noncompliance appears to be almost randomly distributed among the SDOTs and transit agencies. An analysis of fiscal, political, and institutional factors—such as budget size, terms of appointments of agency heads, and agency structure—might yield other results.

CHAPTER 3

Findings and Applications

State Departments of Transportation

SDOTs are the state counterparts to USDOT. Unlike transit agencies, which can be public or private, SDOTs are government agencies "responsible for owning, planning, designing, constructing, operating, maintaining, and repairing major components of each state's transportation system" (3). Originally established in the early 20th century as agencies to plan, design, build, and maintain state and federal highway networks, today SDOTs' responsibilities include aviation, highways, public transportation, waterways, and intermodal programs.

This expanded mission has brought about a change in the composition of the SDOT workforce. When SDOTs were focused on highway construction and maintenance, their ranks were filled with engineers and technicians. Today they employ a broad range of specialists, including planners, architects, environmental scientists, economists, and lawyers (3). A benchmarking study prepared for the Indiana DOT found that, on average, 44% of employees are administrators, managers, or professionals; 32% are technical or craft certified; and 27% are clerical or unskilled (3).

In addition to trying to recruit for a broader range of disciplines, SDOTs also face the challenge of an aging workforce. About 50% of the SDOT workforce will be eligible to retire within the next 10 years, leaving many vacant positions to be filled (3). The pool of prospective employees is more diverse than ever, and SDOTs must think of ways to recruit and retain a workforce that will reflect demographic trends.

Findings

Compliance

Compliance with EEO guidelines can effectively be promoted through communication and enforcement of regulations, as well as through the communication and enforcement of agency-wide goals addressing diversity. SDOTs are making efforts to employ a diverse workforce, as evidenced by their high level of compliance with EEO laws and their submittals of EEO-4 reports.

SDOTs have a twofold responsibility—first, to not exclude women and minorities, and second, to take steps to attract and retain women and minorities. This latter responsibility involves implementing an affirmative action plan and completing an EEO-4 report.

The EEO reporting requirements for SDOTs are set forth in Subpart C of the Equal Employment Opportunity on Federal and Federal-Aid Construction Contracts regulation (17). The purpose of the regulation is to "set forth Federal Highway Administration (FHWA) Federal-aid policy and FHWA and State responsibilities relative to a State highway agency's internal equal employment opportunity program and for assuring compliance with the equal employment opportunity requirements of federally assisted highway construction contracts."

The regulation goes on to state:

> Each State highway agency shall prepare and submit an updated equal employment opportunity program, one year from the date of approval of the preceding program by the Federal Highway Administrator, over the signature of the head of the State highway agency, to the Federal Highway Administrator through the FHWA Division Administrator. (16)

FHWA provided the research team with files containing affirmative action plans and EEO-4 reports submitted by the SDOTs. The EEO-4 report (Form 164) provides information on employees of state and local governments by job category, race, and salary range (17). SDOTs are instructed to use the form to report employment data, and the data are to "reflect only State departments of transportation/State highway department employment" (16). Form FHWA-1392, Federal-Aid Highway Construction Summary of Employment Data, is supposed to "reflect the total employment on all Federal-Aid Highway Projects in the state as of July 31st" (16).

A review of the files provided by FHWA found that not all SDOTs had submitted an EEO-4 report. After follow-up phone calls were made to those agencies that had not submitted a report, the research team had a full set of EEO-4 reports for the SDOTs. The team decided, however, not to include this second batch of reports in the analysis in the belief that establishing a baseline should involve not only an analysis of the data, but also an analysis of the process for collecting and reporting the data. SDOTs are required to submit their affirmative action plans and EEO-4 forms to FHWA annually (*16*). If FHWA does not have an SDOT's EEO-4 report on file, that indicates a process issue (e.g., the SDOT did not submit the form, or the form was submitted but not properly filed).

Comprehensiveness

The federal regulations governing the development of EEO programs instruct SDOTs to produce a comprehensive report.

> The scope of an EEO program and an AAP [affirmative action plan] must be comprehensive, covering all elements of the agency's personnel management policies and practices. The major part of an AAP must be recognition and removal of any barriers to equal employment opportunity, identification of problem areas and of persons unfairly excluded or held back and action enabling them to compete for jobs on an equal basis. An effective AAP not only benefits those who have been denied equal employment opportunity but will also greatly benefit the organization which often has overlooked, screened out or underutilized the great reservoir of untapped human resources and skills, especially among women and minority groups. (*16*)

More specifically, the regulations state that an affirmative action plan should include the following components:

- A strong agency policy statement of commitment to EEO.
- Assignment of responsibility and authority for the program to a qualified individual.
- A survey of the labor market area in terms of population makeup, skills, and availability for employment.
- An analysis of the current workforce to identify jobs, departments, and units where minorities and women are underutilized.
- Specific, measurable, attainable hiring and promotion goals, with target dates, in each area of underutilization.
- Managers and supervisors who are responsible and accountable for meeting these goals.
- Reevaluation of job descriptions and hiring criteria to ensure they reflect actual job needs.
- Identification of minorities and women who are qualified or qualifiable to fill jobs.
- A strategy to get minorities and women into upward mobility and relevant training programs to which they have not previously had access.
- Systems to regularly monitor and measure progress, and if the results are not satisfactory, to determine why and make necessary changes.
- A procedure that allows employees and applicants to submit allegations of discrimination to an impartial body, without fear of reprisal.

The research team was primarily interested in the number of women and minorities employed in SDOTs and transit agencies in relation to their availability in the labor market; hence, the team specifically sought information on the utilization and availability of women and minorities. A review of the SDOT files found that 30 of the 52 SDOTs provided a comprehensive report that included both incumbency numbers (utilization numbers) and availability numbers; this means that an availability analysis, which is a required element of the annual affirmative action plan, was conducted by 58% of the SDOTs.

According to the regulations, SDOTs should, as a minimum, report data for

- The total population in the state;
- The total labor market in the state, with a breakdown by racial/ethnic identification and gender; and
- An analysis of the total population and total labor market in connection with the availability of personnel and jobs within the SDOT.

An availability analysis serves as the basis for determining where there is an underutilization or a concentration of a particular race/ethnic group or gender. It is what allows an agency to establish a legally defensible hiring goal.

In conducting an availability analysis, it is important to collect availability information not only on the total number of minorities, but also on each racial/gender group. For example, a finding that women overall are not underutilized or underrepresented in a particular occupation could be misleading if one group is skewing the results; White women could be overrepresented in that category, while Black or Hispanic women are underrepresented—facts that will be obscured when the data are looked at only in the aggregate.

A comprehensive report will, in addition to providing availability information, also include targeted goals for women and minorities in specific occupational categories. When asked if they set goals or targets for minorities and women,

- Eighty-nine percent of the SDOTs said they have goals or targets for the percentage of women in their workforce; 72% stated that these goals are linked to particular job classifications;
- More than 67% of the SDOTs that have targets for women in particular job classifications have a clear policy of

hiring women in high-skill jobs (officials and administrators, 67%; professionals, 72%; and technicians, 78%);
- Seventy-eight percent of the respondents said their agency has goals for the percentage of minorities they seek to employ, with 67% stating that these goals are linked to particular job classifications; and
- Seventy-one percent of the SDOTs that have targets for minorities in particular job classifications have a clear policy of hiring minorities in high-skill jobs (officials and administrators, 72%; professionals, 86%; and technicians, 86%).

It is important that agencies have specific, rather than general, hiring goals. It is not enough for an agency to state that it wants to increase the percentage of women or minorities in its employ, as this could simply mean hiring more women and minorities in lower level positions. Affirmative action is not just about increasing the number of women and minorities in the workforce; it is also about expanding the opportunities for advancement. An affirmative action program that yields an increase in the numbers of women and minorities employed at an agency, but the women are concentrated in clerical positions and the minorities in service jobs, should not be considered a success. Success means having a diverse workforce throughout the organization, from the top to the bottom; one way to achieve this is to have a comprehensive affirmative action plan with targeted goals that are based on a thorough availability and utilization analysis.

Consistency

To allow meaningful comparisons, data must be presented in a consistent format. In reviewing SDOT and transit agency files, the research team found inconsistencies in the way the data were reported (among SDOTs, among transit agencies, and between SDOTs and transit agencies). The inconsistencies centered around the following issues:

- Date of the availability data. While most agencies used data from the 2000 U.S. Census, four SDOTs used data from the 1990 U.S. Census.
- Source of the availability data. Some agencies used data from the Census, while others used data from state employment agencies.
- Measures of underrepresentation and adverse impact. The SDOTs that provided a workforce analysis used different measures to determine underrepresentation or adverse impact. The measures included employment parity, economic parity, and the four-fifths rule, which states that a selection rate for any racial/ethnic or gender group that is more than four-fifths of the rate for the group with the highest selection rate will generally not be regarded as evidence of adverse impact (4).
- Geographic and organizational units to assess representation. Some SDOTs determine representation status or adverse impact at the district level, while others do so at the state or agency level.
- Racial/ethnic categories used to report employment counts. Some agencies do not distinguish between Hispanic and non-Hispanic; others report numbers for women and minorities, but not for individual racial/ethnic groups.

The data that agencies use for the availability analysis should not only be the most recent, accurate, and relevant data available, but it should also be cross-classified by race and gender to "ascertain the extent to which minority-group women or minority-group men may be underutilized" (15). Just over half of the SDOTs that reported availability data disaggregated their data in a consistent manner (i.e., by race and gender).

Availability numbers are used to calculate underutilization, or disproportionality. The research team used Census data to independently calculate availability rates and then compared the rates with those reported by the SDOTs; any discrepancies might be the result of different sources for availability numbers (i.e., Census data, state employment agency data, other sources).

Confidence

The web survey asked each SDOT to indicate its level of confidence in the accuracy of its utilization and availability analysis.

- Fifty-eight percent of the survey respondents indicated that they are extremely confident in the accuracy of their agency's EEO reports.
- Forty-two percent indicated that they are somewhat confident.

For an agency to have confidence in its data, the data should be updated regularly, and agencies should have computer systems that will allow them to easily track applicants, new hires, and promotions. The web survey found that 65% of respondents update their affirmative action plans annually; 15% update their plans "as needed," 10% update biannually, 5% update quarterly, and 5% update monthly. Some states reported making substantial changes to their plan after each Census.

Establishing the Baseline

To determine the baseline for diversity in SDOTs, the research team sought answers to the following questions:

- What is the disproportionality rate (underutilization or overutilization) of women and minorities within each of the EEO-4 occupational categories?
- What percentage of agencies have an underutilization or overutilization of women and minorities within each of the EEO-4 occupational categories?

The following steps were taken to calculate disproportionality rates:

1. Review the EEO-4 reports and affirmative action plans that the SDOTs submitted to FHWA.
2. Enter the incumbency numbers (number of employees for each racial/gender category) reported by each SDOT into a database.
3. Calculate the utilization rates for women and minorities by dividing the incumbency numbers by the total number of employees. For example, if an SDOT had 10 White female employees and 50 total employees, the utilization rate for White women would be 20%. The utilization rate is calculated separately for Black men and women, Hispanic men and women, Asian men and women, American Indian men and women, and White women.
4. Access the Census Bureau's database to collect the EEO-1 employment counts for women and minorities in each of the seven EEO-4 job categories (an eighth category—paraprofessionals—is not included in this analysis as comparison data are not available from the Census Bureau); these counts will be used to calculate availability rates when an SDOT has not done so.
5. Collect the availability numbers for women and minorities for each of the EEO job categories (officials and administrators, professionals, technicians, protective service workers, administrative support, skilled craft workers, and service-maintenance).
6. Calculate the availability rate for women and minorities by dividing the number of women and minorities by the total number of available workers for each job category.
7. Calculate the disproportionality (underutilization or overutilization) by dividing the utilization rate by the availability rate. For example, if an SDOT's utilization rate for White women in professional and administrative occupations is 20% and the availability rate for White women in those occupations in the general labor market, as reported by the U.S. Census Bureau, is 40%, then the disproportionality is 50% (20/40). There is no disparity if the ratio is at least 80%. In this example, however, the ratio is less than 80%, so there is a disparity. The closer the ratio is to 80%, the smaller the disparity.
8. Identify the job categories and racial/ethnic groups that account for the highest disparity based on the percentage of SDOTs that had a disparity and on the average disparity ratio across the SDOTs, using the four-fifths rule. According to the four-fifths rule, a selection rate for any race or gender that is more than 80% of the rate for the group with the highest selection rate will generally not be regarded as evidence of adverse impact (4).

Overall Findings

The overall disproportionality rates for women and minority employees in SDOTs are shown in Table 2. On average,

- White men are overutilized in all seven occupational categories except protective services and administrative support categories;
- Black men are overutilized in all seven occupational categories;
- White women are underutilized in five of the seven occupational categories (officials and administrators, professionals, technicians, protective service workers, and service-maintenance);
- Black women are underutilized in four occupational categories (professionals, technicians, protective service workers, and service-maintenance);
- Hispanic men are underutilized in five occupational categories (officials and administrators, protective service workers, administrative support, skilled craft workers, and service-maintenance);
- Hispanic women are underutilized in four categories (officials and administrators, professionals, skilled craft workers, and service-maintenance);
- Asian men are overutilized in all categories except for technicians and service-maintenance;
- Asian women are underutilized in all occupational categories except for administrative support;
- American Indian men are overutilized in all categories except protective service workers and administrative support; and
- American Indian women are underutilized in four categories (officials and administrators, professionals, skilled craft workers, and service-maintenance).

The regional disproportionality analyses for women and minority employees in SDOTs are shown in Tables 3–6.

SDOT Disproportionality Analysis by Race Ethnicity and Gender

On average, White men

- Are overutilized in all occupational categories except protective services and administrative support;
- In the Northeast region, are underutilized in protective service workers and in the administrative support categories and overutilized in all other categories except skilled craft;

Table 2. Overall Disproportionality Rates for Women and Minorities in SDOTs.

	Officials/ Administrators (%)	Professionals (%)	Technicians (%)	Protective Service Workers (%)	Administrative Support (%)	Skilled Craft Workers (%)	Service- Maintenance (%)
White Males	130	169	111	98	83	102	205
White Females	41	39	55	65	88	87	21
Black Males	122	141	166	273	138	295	156
Black Females	345	49	74	42	110	92	27
Hispanic Males	73	159	140	65	48	44	74
Hispanic Females	21	38	80	80	84	27	9
Asian Males	100	149	36	117	102	134	28
Asian Females	30	70	28	13	83	12	9
American Indian Males	182	344	317	68	51	118	249
American Indian Females	18	68	298	612	126	74	14

NOTE: > 100% = overutilization; 80% = parity; < 80% = underutilization
Source: SDOT Utilization Data and U.S. Census Bureau

Table 3. Disproportionality Analysis for State DOTs—Northeast Region.

	Officials/ Administrators (%)	Professionals (%)	Technicians (%)	Protective Service Workers (%)	Administrative Support (%)	Skilled Craft Workers (%)	Service- Maintenance (%)
White Males	125	166	120	64	76	89	205
White Females	36	31	35	22	81	58	13
Black Males	24	130	211	1275	39	72	132
Black Females	120	40	172	0	113	27	17
Hispanic Males	59	46	23	10	19	32	50
Hispanic Females	22	20	17	0	64	8	18
Asian Males	26	219	4	0	24	77	28
Asian Females	17	30	17	0	28	0	0
American Indian Males	0	521	312	0	33	76	198
American Indian Females	0	62	34	0	69	47	0

NOTE: >100% = overutilization; 80% = parity; <80% = underutilization
Source: SDOT Utilization Data and U.S. Census Bureau
Northeast Region = Connecticut, Maine, Massachusetts, New Hampshire, Rhode Island, Vermont, New Jersey, New York, and Pennsylvania.

Table 4. Disproportionality Analysis for SDOTs—Midwest Region.

	Officials/ Administrators (%)	Professionals (%)	Technicians (%)	Protective Service Workers (%)	Administrative Support (%)	Skilled Craft Workers (%)	Service-Maintenance (%)
White Males	129	191	129	95	61	105	253
White Females	46	41	52	115	91	81	15
Black Males	140	141	132	53	142	638	112
Black Females	45	37	49	55	80	58	14
Hispanic Males	126	200	144	111	62	43	79
Hispanic Females	15	63	94	83	131	24	2
Asian Males	126	86	14	143	137	83	24
Asian Females	71	80	11	64	92	0	1
American Indian Males	502	372	420	88	12	161	257
American Indian Females	32	82	454	725	299	0	3

NOTE: >100% = overutilization; 80% = parity; <80% = underutilization
Source: SDOT Utilization Data and U.S. Census Bureau
Midwest Region = Indiana, Illinois, Michigan, Ohio, Wisconsin, Iowa, Kansas, Minnesota, Missouri, Nebraska, North Dakota, and South Dakota

Table 5. Disproportionality Analysis for SDOTs—Southern Region.

	Officials/ Administrators (%)	Professionals (%)	Technicians (%)	Protective Service Workers (%)	Administrative Support (%)	Skilled Craft Workers (%)	Service-Maintenance (%)
White Males	136	169	115	107	84	110	180
White Females	41	41	47	41	89	94	25
Black Males	110	187	189	165	208	339	165
Black Females	46	52	64	66	116	124	27
Hispanic Males	27	106	68	37	31	27	32
Hispanic Females	7	29	47	23	35	14	6
Asian Males	58	115	29	28	90	116	11
Asian Females	8	62	9	0	73	18	15
American Indian Males	105	318	252	89	64	81	277
American Indian Females	16	72	315	577	67	90	26

NOTE: >100% = overutilization; 80% = parity; <80% = underutilization
Source: SDOT Utilization Data and U.S. Census Bureau
Southern Region = Delaware, District of Columbia, Florida, Georgia, Maryland, North Carolina, South Carolina, Virginia, West Virginia, Alabama, Kentucky, Mississippi, Tennessee, Arkansas, Louisiana, Oklahoma, and Texas

Table 6. Disproportionality Analysis for SDOTs—Western Region.

	Officials/ Administrators (%)	Professionals (%)	Technicians (%)	Protective Service Workers (%)	Administrative Support (%)	Skilled Craft Workers (%)	Service- Maintenance (%)
White Males	125	149	87	104	105	95	200
White Females	41	41	79	89	88	109	25
Black Males	176	84	135	60	92	89	191
Black Females	1110[a]	57	53	0	125	107	43
Hispanic Males	105	261	298	106	78	74	141
Hispanic Females	43	42	156	246	127	59	13
Asian Males	176	209	80	341	132	231	57
Asian Females	35	94	77	0	119	22	12
American Indian Males	139	262	325	49	72	155	233
American Indian Females	21	55	260	22	105	127	15

NOTE: >100% = overutilization; 80% = parity; <80% = underutilization
Source: SDOT Utilization Data and U.S. Census Bureau
Western Region = Arizona, Colorado, Idaho, New Mexico, Montana, Utah, Nevada, Wyoming, Alaska, California, Hawaii, Oregon, and Washington

- In the Midwest region, are underutilized in the administrative support category and overutilized in all other categories except protective services;
- In the Southern region, are overutilized in all occupational categories except administrative support;
- In the Western region, are overutilized in all occupational categories except the technicians and skilled craft categories.

On average, White women

- Are underutilized in five of the seven occupational categories (officials and administrators, professionals, technicians, protective service workers, and service-maintenance);
- In the Northeast region, are underutilized in all occupational categories except administrative support;
- In the Midwest region, are underutilized in four categories (officials and administrators, professionals, technicians and service-maintenance);
- In the Southern region, are underutilized in all occupational categories except administrative support and skilled craft workers; and
- In the Western region, are underutilized in three categories (officials/administrators, professionals, and service-maintenance).

On average, Black men

- Are overutilized in all occupational categories;
- In the Northeast region, are underutilized in the categories of officials and administrators, administrative support, and skilled craft workers;
- In the Midwest region, are underrepresented in the protective service workers category;
- In the Southern region, are overrepresented in all occupational categories; and
- In the Western region, are underrepresented in the protective services category.

On average, Black women

- Are underutilized in the professionals, technicians, protective service workers, and service-maintenance occupational categories;
- In the Northeast region, are underutilized in the professionals, protective service workers, skilled craft workers, and service-maintenance categories;
- In the Midwest region, are underutilized in all occupational categories except administrative support;
- In the Southern region, are underutilized in all occupational categories except administrative support and skilled craft workers; and
- In the Western region, are overutilized in the administrative support and skilled craft workers categories.

On average, Hispanic men

- Are underutilized in all occupational categories except professionals and technicians;

- In the Northeast region, are underutilized in all occupational categories;
- In the Midwest region, are overutilized in the officials and administrators, professionals, technicians, and protective service workers categories and underutilized in the administrative support, skilled craft workers, and service-maintenance categories;
- In the Southern region, are underutilized in all occupational categories except professionals; and
- In the Western region, are overutilized in all occupational categories except administrative support and skilled craft workers.

On average, Hispanic women

- Are underutilized in the categories of officials and administrators, professionals, skilled craft workers, and service-maintenance;
- In the Northeast region, are underutilized in all occupational categories;
- In the Midwest region, are underutilized in the officials and administrators, professionals, skilled craft workers, and service-maintenance categories;
- In the Southern region, are underutilized in all occupational categories; and
- In the Western region, are underutilized in the categories of officials and administrators, professionals, skilled craft workers, and service-maintenance.

On average, Asian men

- Are overutilized in all occupational categories except technicians and service-maintenance;
- In the Northeast region, are underutilized in all occupational categories except professionals;
- In the Midwest region, are overutilized in all occupational categories except technicians and service-maintenance;
- In the Southern region, are underutilized in the categories of officials and administrators, technicians, protective service workers, and service-maintenance; and
- In the Western region, are overutilized in all occupational categories except service-maintenance.

On average, Asian women

- Are inderutilized in all occupational categories except technicians;
- In the Northeast region, are underutilized in all occupational categories;
- In the Midwest region, are underutilized in all occupational categories except professionals and administrative support;
- In the Southern region, are underutilized in all occupational categories; and
- In the Western region, are underutilized in all occupational categories except professionals and administrative support.

On average, American Indian men

- Are overutilized in all occupational categories except protective services workers and administrative support;
- In the Northeast region, are underutilized in the categories of officials and administrators, protective service workers, administrative support, and skilled craft workers;
- In the Midwest region, are overutilized in all occupational categories except administrative support;
- In the Southern region, are overutilized in all occupational categories except administrative support; and
- In the Western region, are overutilized in all occupational categories except protective service workers and administrative support.

On average, American Indian women

- Are underutilized in the officials and administrators, professionals, skilled craft workers, and service-maintenance categories;
- In the Northeast region, are underutilized in all occupational categories;
- In the Midwest region, are overutilized in the professionals, technicians, protective service workers, and administrative support categories;
- In the Southern region, are underutilized in the officials and administrators, professionals, administrative support, and service-maintenance categories; and
- In the Western region, are overutilized in the technicians, administrative support, and skilled craft workers categories and underutilized in the officials and administrators, professionals, protective service workers, and service-maintenance categories.

SDOT Disproportionality Analysis by Region

In the Northeast region,

- All groups are underutilized in the skilled craft workers occupational category except white men;
- White women are underutilized in all occupational categories except administrative support;
- Black women are overutilized in the administrative support category;
- All groups of men are overutilized in the professionals category; and
- All groups, except for Black women, are underutilized in the officials and administrators category.

In the Midwest region,

- All groups of men are overutilized in the officials and administrators and professionals categories;
- All groups of women are underutilized in the officials and administrators and service-maintenance categories; and

- American Indian men are overutilized in all categories except administrative support.

In the Southern region,

- White men are overutilized in all occupational categories except administrative support;
- Black men are overutilized in all occupational categories;
- Hispanic women are underutilized in all occupational categories;
- Asian women are underutilized in all occupational categories;
- All groups of women are underutilized in the officials and administrators and the technicians categories; and
- All groups of men are overutilized in the professionals occupational category.

In the Western region,

- White men are overutilized in all occupational categories except protective services and technicians;
- Black men are overutilized in all occupational categories except protective services;
- Hispanic women are underutilized in the officials and administrators and professionals categories;
- White women are underutilized in the officials and administrators and professionals categories; and
- American Indian women are underutilized in the officials and administrators and professionals categories.

Underutilization of Women and Minorities in SDOTs

Table 7 lists the percentages of SDOTs found to have an underutilization of women and minorities in each of the seven employment categories.

The officials and administrators category has the highest underutilization of women and minorities. Women and minorities, with the exception of Black men, are underutilized in the officials and administrators category by at least 60% of SDOTs; Black men are underutilized by 47%. The officials and administrators category is the highest occupational level, encompassing positions in which administrative and managerial personnel "set broad policies, exercise overall responsibility for execution of these policies, or direct individual departments or special phases of the agency's operations or provide specialized consultation on a regional, district, or area basis"(17). Since this category represents the highest underutilization, agencies should develop succession plans and offer professional development opportunities that will lead to higher numbers of women and minorities in these positions.

The occupational category with the smallest underutilization rate is the protective service workers category, with six of the eight racial/gender groups underutilized by fewer than half the SDOTs.

Hispanic women were underutilized in all seven occupational categories by more than half of the SDOTs. Black women were underutilized by more than half of the SDOTs

Table 7. SDOTs with an Underutilization of Women and Minorities, by Employment Category.

	Officials/ Administrators (%)	Professionals (%)	Technicians (%)	Protective Service Workers (%)	Administrative Support (%)	Skilled Craft Workers (%)	Service-Maintenance (%)
Black Males	47	29	27	31	67	37	41
Black Females	86	82	69	51	41	65	98
Hispanic Males	73	37	55	43	78	84	69
Hispanic Females	92	90	63	53	61	90	98
Asian Males	61	29	90	49	71	59	92
Asian Females	88	61	82	49	53	90	98
American Indian Males	69	31	29	43	82	55	47
American Indian Females	94	69	41	49	65	71	94
White Females	90	96	78	39	22	53	94

NOTE: N = 48 SDOTs.
SOURCE: SDOT EEO-4 reports and U.S. Census.

in all occupational categories but administrative support. White women were underutilized in five categories by more than half of the SDOTs.

Men had the lowest underutilization in the professionals occupational category, with fewer than 40% of the SDOTs underutilizing Black, Hispanic, Asian, or American Indian men in this category.

Women in all racial/ethnic groups evidence the highest underutilization. More than three-fourths of the SDOTs underutilize Black women in three categories—officials and administrators, professionals, and service-maintenance. More than three-fourths of the SDOTs underutilize White women in four categories—officials and administrators, professionals, technicians, and service-maintenance. Hispanic women have the highest level of underutilization by the SDOTs, with nearly all of the SDOTs (more than 90%) underutilizing Hispanic women in four categories—officials and administrators, professionals, skilled craft workers, and service-maintenance.

American Indian women and Asian women are underutilized by more than 90% of the SDOTs in two categories—American Indian women in the officials and administrators and service-maintenance categories, and Asian women in the skilled craft workers and service-maintenance categories.

Nearly all of the SDOTs underutilized the following groups and categories:

- Black women in the service-maintenance occupational category (98%)
- Hispanic women in the officials and administrators category (92%)
- Hispanic women in the professionals category (90%)
- Hispanic women in the service-maintenance category (98%)
- Asian men in the technicians category (90%)
- Asian men in the service-maintenance category (92%)
- American Indian women in the officials and administrators category (94%)
- American Indian women in the service-maintenance category (94%)
- White women in the officials and administrators category (90%)
- White women in the professionals category (96%)
- White women in the service-maintenance category (94%)

Men (Black, Hispanic, Asian, and American Indian) were underutilized in the administrative support category by at least two-thirds of the SDOTs.

Black men were the least underutilized of the eight groups. Fewer than half the SDOTs underutilized Black men in six of the occupational categories (officials and administrators, professionals, technicians, protective service workers, skilled craft workers, and service-maintenance); nearly two-thirds of the SDOTs underutilized Black men in the administrative support category.

As a group, Black women experienced the highest underutilization in the service-maintenance occupational category, with almost all of the states (98%) underutilizing Black women in this occupation. Black women also experienced a high level of underutilization in the categories of officials and administrators (86%), professionals (82%), and technicians (69%).

Hispanic men are primarily underutilized in the administrative support (78%), skilled craft workers (84%), and officials and administrators (73%) categories.

Hispanic women have a high incidence of underutilization in all occupational categories. More than 90% of the SDOTs underutilize Hispanic women in the officials and administrators, professionals, skilled craft workers, and service-maintenance occupational categories. Hispanic women are underutilized in the protective services category by 53% of the SDOTs and by more than 60% of the SDOTs in the technician and administrative support categories.

As a group, Asian men are significantly underutilized in the service-maintenance (92%) and technicians (90%) categories.

The highest occurrences of underutilization of Asian women are in the service-maintenance (98%), skilled craft workers (90%), officials and administrators (88%), and technicians (82%) occupational categories.

The highest incidence of underutilization for American Indian men occurs in the administrative support occupational category (82%).

American Indian women are primarily underutilized in the officials and administrators (94%) and service-maintenance (94%) occupational categories.

White women are primarily underutilized in the professionals (96%), service-maintenance (94%), officials and administrators (90%), and technicians (78%) categories.

Baseline for SDOTs

The research team has developed a preliminary baseline and proposed benchmarks based on the analysis of SDOT files (see Table 8).

This proposed benchmark is a starting point; before a true benchmark for diversity in SDOTs can be established, the following questions should be answered:

- Should SDOTs focus on eliminating all disparities, or focus instead on one or more occupational categories?
- Should SDOTs have a targeted goal?
- Should the goal be to have more women and minorities in top-level positions (officials and administrators), or should the goal be to have more women and minorities throughout the organization?

Table 8. Preliminary Baseline and Proposed Benchmarks for SDOTs.

Baseline	Performance Indicator	Benchmark
• Women in all racial groups are underutilized in the officials and administrators category by more than 80% of SDOTs.	• Reduce the underutilization of females in the officials and administrators category. • Increase the number of women and minorities in the officials and administrators category.	• Women are underutilized in the officials and administrators category by fewer than than 50% of SDOTs.
• Women in all racial groups are underutilized in the professionals category by more than 50% of SDOTs.	• Reduce the underutilization of women in the professionals category.	• Women are underutilized in the professionals occupational category by fewer than 25% of the SDOTs.
• Women in all racial groups are underutilized in the service-maintenance category by more than 90% of SDOTs.	• Reduce the underutilization of women in the service-maintenance category.	• Women are underutilized in the service-maintenance category by less than 50% of SDOTs.
• Black, Hispanic, Asian, and White women are underutilized in the technicians category by more than 50% of SDOTs.	• Reduce the underutilization of Black, Hispanic, Asian, and White women in the technicians category	• Black, Hispanic, Asian, and White women are underutilized in the technicians category by fewer than 25% of SDOTs.
• Black men are underutilized in the officials and administrators category by nearly 50% of SDOTs.	• Reduce the underutilization of Black men in the officials and administrators category.	• Black men are underutilized in the officials and administrators category by fewer than 25% of SDOTs.
• Hispanic, Asian, and American Indian men are underutilized in the officials and administrators category by more than 60% of SDOTs.	• Reduce the underutilization or Hispanic, Asian, and American Indian men in the officials and administrators category.	• Hispanic, Asian, and American Indian men are underutilized in the officials and administrators category by fewer than 50% of SDOTs.
• Hispanic and Asian men are underutilized by more than 50% of SDOTs in the technicians category.	• Reduce the underutilization of Hispanic and Asian men in the technicians category.	• Hispanic and Asian men are underutilized in the technicians category by fewer than 30% of SDOTs.

- Where do SDOTs have the greatest need? Do they need more administrators, engineers, planners, information technology specialists, office support workers, or maintenance workers, or is the need the same for all occupational categories?
- Should an overall baseline be established for all SDOTs, or should separate baselines be established by region, by individual state, or by size of state?

Transit Agencies

Transit agencies provide public transportation services involving buses, subways, light rail, commuter rail, monorail, passenger ferry boats, and trolleys. Unlike SDOTs, which are all state government agencies, transit agencies can be public or private and can have a local or regional focus.

Like SDOTs, transit agencies employ professionals with bachelor's degrees, such as engineers, planners, and information technology specialists; they also employ a large number of workers with high school degrees and with technical certifications, such as entry-level bus operators and mechanics. "The transit workforce comprises approximately 225,000 employees. Of this total, about 58 percent are vehicle operators, 20 percent are assigned to vehicle maintenance, and 12 percent are assigned to nonvehicle maintenance. The balance of the transit workforce is assigned to general administration" (*3*).

The five key job categories that are the most difficult for transit agencies to recruit and retain workers for are bus and train operators, equipment maintenance staff, planners, engineers, and information technology specialists (*18*).

Transit agencies, like SDOTs, receive funding from USDOT. In the case of transit agencies, these funds come in the form of grants from FTA, which are to be used for the development, improvement, maintenance, and operation of new or existing transit systems. FTA is responsible for ensuring the grantees comply with statutory and administrative requirements, and the grantees are responsible for managing their programs in accordance with federal requirements, including the requirement to have a DBE program.

Findings

Compliance

FTA provides its grantees with very detailed and up-to-date guidance on how to develop a DBE program (*12*), but does not provide guidance on how to develop a legally defensible affirmative action plan.

For the purposes of this report, a transit agency was considered in compliance if it submitted an EEO-4 form. Twenty-nine of the 50 transit agencies studied produced some type of EEO-4 information, with 22 of those agencies actually completing an EEO-4 report. Nine agencies either did not provide employment counts by race and gender, or provided data for the EEO categories in a document other than the EEO-4 form. An additional nine transit agencies provided a breakdown by race and gender for more than 50 job categories, but did not combine the data to fit the EEO-4 categories.

Unlike SDOTs, which have a unambiguous requirement to submit an affirmative action plan and EEO-4 form annually, transit agencies have some flexibility and discretion with regard to the submittal of EEO data. "All designated State agencies will maintain and provide data and report to UMTA [FTA] as specified in Chapter III of this circular or at the discretion of the UMTA Area Civil Rights Officer" (*15*).

The Circular goes on to state, "Each applicant, recipient, or subrecipient meeting the EEO circular threshold requirements shall submit to UMTA an updated EEO submission on a triennial basis or as major changes occur in the work force or employment conditions. At the discretion of the UMTA Office of Civil Rights, less information may be requested where the recipient's previously submitted EEO program has not changed significantly." Failure to comply with the terms could result in a determination of noncompliance and the imposition of sanctions.

Comprehensiveness

A transit EEO program must include the following components:

- Statement of policy
- Dissemination mechanisms
- Designation of responsibility to agency personnel
- Utilization analysis
- Goals and timetables
- Assessment of employment practices to identify causes of underutilization
- Monitoring and reporting systems (*15*)

The utilization analysis should consist of a workforce analysis and an availability analysis (*15*). The workforce analysis requires a statistical breakdown of the grant recipient's workforce by each department, job category, grade/rank of employee, and job title, with the data cross-referenced by race, national origin, and gender.

An availability analysis is a comparison of the participation rates of minorities and women at various levels in the workforce with their availability in relevant labor markets. A labor market has both geographic and occupational components. Different geographic areas and labor force data should be used for different job categories. Professional positions, for example, would likely have a regional or national recruiting area, whereas less skilled jobs would likely have a local recruiting area.

FTA provides transit agencies with guidance on how to conduct an availability analysis and suggests potential data sources.

> In determining availability for job categories not requiring special skills or abilities, general population or work force age data may be suitable. Community and area labor statistics by race, national origin, and sex can be obtained from the U.S. Department of Commerce, Bureau of the Census, and its publications; U.S. Department of Labor, Bureau of Labor Statistics, and the Women's Bureau; State and local governments, especially State employment services and MPOs. Detailed occupational data by race, national origin and sex, in categories required for EEO reports ... is available in special affirmative action data packages from many State employment services." (*15*)

Availability data were provided by 16 of the transit agencies.

Consistency

It is easier to require and enforce consistency when dealing with a homogenous group such as SDOTs, as opposed to a heterogeneous group such as transit agencies. Unlike SDOTs, which are all state agencies, transit agencies can be local, state, or regional and public or private. As state agencies, SDOTs have their leaders appointed by the governor. Transit agencies, in contrast, "are usually governed by a board of directors or trustees comprising public citizens appointed by a governor, mayor, or other elected official. Sometimes approval of appointments is also required by a legislative body (the state legislature or the city council). Members typically represent specific political jurisdictions…. The vast majority of transit boards avoid day-to-day operations and focus on policy issues" (3).

There were inconsistencies in the data, both among transit agencies and between transit agencies and SDOTs. The inconsistencies involved the following issues:

- Date the employment counts were collected. Because transit agencies are required to submit affirmative action plans on a triennial basis, the dates of the EEO-4 ranged from 2000 to 2005.
- Date of the availability data. While the majority of agencies used Census 2000 data, reports submitted prior to the availability of the 2000 Census data were based on data from the 1990 Census.
- Job categories used to report employment counts. Not all agencies used the EEO-4 occupational categories. Nine transit agencies provided a breakdown by race and gender for over 50 job categories, but did not consolidate the data into the EEO-4 categories.

Confidence

Transit agencies were not included in the web survey; thus, the research team does not have any measure of how confident those agencies are of their EEO data.

Developing a Baseline

Although the research team performed the same calculation to establish a baseline for transit agencies as it did with SDOTs, there are major limitations in the transit analysis. While the availability pool for an SDOT is usually the entire state, transit agencies, which serve local, state, or regional areas, have different availability pools. If the appropriate pool is not properly identified, the disproportionality rates for transit agencies could be over- or underestimated.

Overall Findings

The overall disproportionality rates for transit agencies are shown in Table 9. On average,

- White men are overutilized in all of the occupational categories;
- Black men are overutilized in all of the occupational categories;

Table 9. Overall Disproportionality Rates for Transit Agencies.

	Officials/ Administrators (%)	Professionals (%)	Technicians (%)	Protective Service Workers (%)	Administrative Support (%)	Skilled Craft Workers (%)	Service-Maintenance (%)
White Males	185	210	251	272	195	190	279
White Females	27	35	36	42	33	22	12
Black Males	185	210	251	272	195	190	279
Black Females	103	150	191	237	192	158	131
Hispanic Males	62	73	85	66	64	40	84
Hispanic Females	23	41	37	61	55	163	28
Asian Males	91	45	43	30	118	183	81
Asian Females	86	18	12	100	43	7	9
American Indian Males	16	103	55	0	101	67	120
American Indian Females	41	20	48	0	45	86	47

NOTES: N = 31 agencies. > 80% = overutilization; 80% = parity; < 80% = underutilization

Table 10. Transit Agencies with an Underutilization of Women and Minorities, by Employment Category.

	Officials/ Administrators (%)	Professionals (%)	Technicians (%)	Protective Service Workers (%)	Administrative Support (%)	Skilled Craft Workers (%)	Service-Maintenance (%)
Black Males	47	41	38	34	44	41	38
Black Females	56	38	53	38	38	63	56
Hispanic Males	69	63	69	34	66	75	72
Hispanic Females	84	75	75	44	72	84	91
Asian Males	69	75	75	50	72	50	72
Asian Females	81	91	88	47	75	84	100
American Indian Males	91	81	88	53	81	75	56
American Indian Females	88	88	72	47	81	66	78
White Females	91	81	75	47	88	91	100

NOTE: N = 31.

- White women are underutilized in all of the occupational categories;
- Black women are overutilized in all of the occupational categories;
- Hispanic men are underutilized in five of the seven occupational categories (officials and administrators, professionals, protective service workers, administrative support, and skilled craft workers);
- Hispanic women are underutilized in all of the occupational categories except for skilled craft workers;
- Asian men are overutilized in four occupational categories (officials and administrators, administrative support, skilled craft workers, and service-maintenance);
- Asian women are underutilized in all of the occupational categories except for officials and administrators and protective service workers;
- American Indian men are underutilized in officials and administrators, technicians, protective service workers, and skilled craft workers; and
- American Indian women are underutilized in all of the occupational categories except skilled craft workers.

There is a disparity between the utilization and availability of women and minorities in most of the transit agencies included in this study. The occupational categories that have the highest underutilization of women and minorities are officials and administrators, professionals, technicians, and service-maintenance. More than half of the transit agencies in this study evidenced a disparity between utilization and availability of all racial/gender groups, with the exception of Black men and women, in these occupational categories (Table 10).

The smallest underutilization was found in the protective services category.

At least half of the agencies underutilize Asian and American Indian men in all the occupational categories.

White and Hispanic women were underutilized in six of the seven occupational categories by more than 70% of the transit agencies in the study.

The least underutilized group appears to be Black men, with fewer than half of the transit agencies in this study reporting an underutilization of Black men.

Nearly all of the transit agencies underutilized the following groups:

- White women in the officials and administrators occupational category (91%)
- White women in the skilled craft workers category (91%)
- White women in the service-maintenance category (100%)
- Hispanic women in the service-maintenance category (91%)
- Asian women in the professional category (91%)
- Asian women in the service-maintenance occupational category (100%)
- American Indian men in the officials and administrators category (91%)

Although Black men are underutilized in transit agencies, relative to the other eight groups they were the least

Table 11. Preliminary Baseline and Proposed Benchmarks for Transit Agencies.

Baseline	Performance Indicator	Benchmark
- All minority groups except Black men are underutilized in the officials and administrators occupational category by more than half of the top-50 transit agencies.	- Reduce the underutilization of minorities and women in the officials and administrators occupational category. - Increase the number of women in minorities in the officials and administrators category.	- Minorities and women will be underutilized by fewer than 25% of the top-50 transit agencies.
- Hispanic and Asian women are underutilized in six of the seven occupational categories by more than 70% of the top-50 transit agencies.	- Reduce the underutilization of Hispanic and Asian women. - Increase the number of Hispanic and Asian women in the officials and administrators, professionals, technicians, administrative support, skilled craft workers, and service-maintenance categories	- Hispanic and Asian women are underutilized by fewer than half of the top-50 transit agencies
- Asian men are underutilized in all seven occupational categories by 50% or more of the top-50 transit agencies.	- Reduce the underutilization of Asian men. - Increase the number of Asian men in all seven occupational categories.	- Asian males are underutilized by less than 25% of the top-50 transit agencies
- American Indian men are underutilized by 75% or more of the top-50 transit agencies in five occupational categories (officials and administrators, professionals, technicians, administrative support, and skilled craft workers).	- Reduce the underutilization of American Indian men. - Increase the number of American Indian men in the officials and administrators, professionals, technicians, administrative support, and skilled craft workers categories.	- American Indian men are underutilized by fewer than 50% of the top-50 transit agencies.
- White women are underutilized in six of the seven occupational categories by more than 75% of the top-50 transit agencies.	- Decrease the underutilization rate for White women. - Increase the number of White females in the officials and administrators, professionals, technicians, administrative support, skilled craft workers, and service-maintenance occupational categories.	- White women are underutilized by fewer than 50% of the top-50 transit agencies.

underutilized group; this was also the case in SDOTs. Black men were underutilized by less than half of the transit agencies, in all occupational categories.

As a group, Black women experienced their highest level of underutilization in the skilled craft workers occupational category (63%), followed by the officials and administrators and service-maintenance categories (56% each).

Sixty percent or more of the transit agencies in this study had an underutilization of Hispanic men in nearly all of the occupational categories—officials and administrators (69%), professionals (63%), technicians (69%), administrative support (66%), skilled craft workers (75%), and service-maintenance (72%).

Seventy percent or more of the transit agencies had an underutilization of Hispanic women in all but one occupational category (protective service workers).

At least half of the transit agencies had an underutilization of Asian men in all the occupational categories—officials and administrators (69%), professionals (75%), technicians (75%), protective service workers (50%), administrative support (72%), skilled craft workers (50%), and service-maintenance (72%).

Seventy-five percent or more of the transit agencies in the study had an underutilization of Asian women in nearly all the occupational categories—officials and administrators (81%), professionals (91%), technicians (88%), administrative support (75%), skilled craft workers (84%), and service-maintenance (100%).

Seventy-five percent or more of the transit agencies in the study had an underutilization of American Indian males in the officials and administrators (91%), professionals (81%), technicians (88%), administrative support (81%), and skilled craft workers (75%) categories.

Seventy percent or more of the transit agencies had an underutilization of American Indian women in the officials and administrators (88%), professionals (88%), technicians (72%), administrative support (81%), and service-maintenance (78%) categories.

Seventy-five percent or more of the transit agencies had an underutilization of White women in nearly all occupational categories—officials and administrators (91%), professionals (81%), technicians (75%), administrative support (88%), skilled craft (91%), and service-maintenance (100%).

The average disparity ratio was used to develop the baseline shown in Table 11. Proposed benchmarks for transit agencies are also shown in Table 11.

CHAPTER 4

Conclusions and Recommendations

Conclusions

- Not all SDOTs and transit agencies file EEO-4 reports and FHWA-1392 forms to record their progress in achieving EEO goals.
- SDOTs and transit agencies report their EEO information in inconsistent formats, making analysis difficult.
- Not all SDOTs and transit agencies conduct comprehensive availability analyses. A large number of agencies do not report availability information. Some agencies that do report availability information provide the information only in the aggregate, which precludes agencies from determining which racial/ethnic groups and occupational categories are underutilized and from developing narrowly tailored and legally defensible hiring goals.
- The employment tracking systems used by SDOTs and transit agencies are insufficient to instill confidence in the EEO data produced by the agencies.
- Agencies are given little incentive to submit EEO data.

Recommendations

The research team proposes five key recommendations based on the four elements of the conceptual framework (compliance, consistency, comprehensiveness, and confidence) and on a fifth element, consequences, which surfaced as a result of the analysis.

Make It Easier for Agencies to Be Compliant

A process should be developed to enable SDOTs and transit agencies to submit their EEO-4 and FHWA-1392 data electronically. This would allow for more efficient data collection and would improve the data analysis.

SDOTs and transit agencies should ensure employment information is regularly and accurately recorded.

Provide Standardized Training and Facilitate the Sharing of Information and Best Practices Among Agencies

SDOT and transit agency staff responsible for EEO reporting should be properly trained on how to develop and maintain an effective EEO program. Staff should be accorded time away from their regular duties to attend training sessions.

In *The Workforce Challenge*, the authors recommend that training be a key priority for all transportation agencies and that training be viewed as an investment. They note that successful organizations spend at least four times as much as do transportation agencies on training, and they suggest that transportation agencies consider an "investment goal of 2 percent of salaries for training," which is "equivalent to about 40 hours of training annually for each employee" (*3*).

SDOTs and transit agencies also need opportunities for sharing their best practices regarding the development and monitoring of diversity goals (for a discussion of best practices, see Appendix E). One means that SDOTs currently have for sharing best practices is through postings on the Transportation Workforce Development website (www.nhi.fhwa.dot.gov/transworkforce/innovative.asp). For example, one current posting in the Innovative Practices for State DOT Workforce Management section of the site describes how the New Hampshire DOT "used an ACCESS software database to create a tracking system that analyzes various stages of its internal hiring and selection process" (www.nhi.fhwa.dot.gov/transworkforce/IP_NH.PDF).

The NHDOT staff found that the database they developed helps them save valuable time when filling a job vacancy. It allows them to track an application's progress through the system and to identify where improvements could make the process more efficient.

As a result of the benchmarking process, NHDOT learned that the impediments were "the time lost in manually transferring paperwork through messenger and mail systems" and "the time between when the Bureau posted vacancy announcements and coordinated candidate reviews." NHDOT now has a baseline from which to measure its progress. The result has been a 50% reduction in the time needed to process job vacancies.

Communicate the Key Elements of an Effective Affirmative Action Plan

SDOTs and transit agencies should incorporate an availability analysis in their affirmative action plan. It is important that agencies have a comprehensive affirmative action plan that includes both a utilization analysis and an availability analysis, as well as a report on areas of underutilization, an analysis of applicant flow, the establishment of short- and long-range hiring goals, and strategies for achieving those goals. The information in the plan should be disaggregated (i.e., provided for each racial/ethnic group, cross-referenced by gender), and each racial/ethnic group should be analyzed separately.

The utilization analysis will identify racial/gender groups that are underutilized and allow agencies to establish targeted goals. The availability rate should be calculated using Census data, as well as data reflecting actual applicant flow; the latter will provide a more narrowly tailored applicant pool.

To Promote Greater Accuracy, Agencies Should Improve Internal Monitoring and Tracking Systems

Funds should be made available to allow SDOTs and transit agencies to improve their internal reporting, monitoring, and tracking systems. It is no secret that successful agencies monitor results. "Companies must consider more than the numerical mix of various demographic groups in the workforce. As a rule, whatever gets measured in corporations gets done, so defining metrics and tracking progress are critical to keeping management attention focused on the issue" (19).

In Canada, internal monitoring is a characteristic of government agencies that have been successful in their diversity efforts:

> Departments and agencies with strong leadership and "ownership" of Embracing Change, are generally more successful . . . . These organizations typically adopt measures such as active internal monitoring and discussion of progress at executive tables . . . focussed strategies to move visible minorities into executive ranks, investment in recruitment and development programs, and support for visible minority networks. (20)

SDOTs and transit agencies should monitor and track applicants, hires, and promotions by race and gender so they can prepare detailed reports that will allow them to identify occupations where there is an underutilization of women and minorities and to establish narrowly tailored goals.

Make Diversity an Agency Priority by Holding Everyone Accountable for Achieving Diversity Goals

SDOTs and transit agencies should hold everyone, staff and leadership alike, accountable for achieving diversity and affirmative action goals. Traditionally, it has been one office, whether it be personnel/human resources or affirmative action, that has been responsible for developing, coordinating, and reviewing diversity and affirmative action policies and initiatives, as well as for collecting, reporting, and monitoring diversity and affirmative action goals. That is no longer sufficient; there needs to be commitment from everyone in the organization.

According to FTA, affirmative action programs are to be managed by an executive who reports directly to the agency's CEO, as evidence of the importance of the program to the agency.

> The importance of an EEO program is indicated by the individual the agency has named to manage the program and the authority this individual possesses. An executive should be appointed as Manager/Director of EEO who reports and is directly responsible to the agency's chief executive officer. Since managing the EEO program requires a major commitment of time and resources, the Manager/Director of EEO should be given top management support and assigned a staff commensurate with the importance of this program. (15)

Diversity and affirmative action efforts should cross racial, gender, ethnic, and occupational lines. In the article, "Creating Status of Women Reports: Institutional Housekeeping as 'Women's Work,'" the authors discuss how committees that collect, analyze, and interpret data associated with recruiting, retaining, and promoting female students and faculty have traditionally been staffed by female members of the faculty (21). The authors argue that institutions also need to take responsibility for improving the status of women.

Academia is not alone in recognizing the need for institutional responsibility; the transit industry has also acknowledged that it is imperative that the entire organization take responsibility for diversity and affirmative action goals. As stated in FTA's guidelines:

> Although the agency's EEO program manager has primary responsibility for implementing agency's EEO plan, carrying out EEO and affirmative action is an integral function of all officials, managers and supervisors. Management—from the supervisor of the smallest unit to the chairman of the board or chief executive officer—bears the responsibility of ensuring that the agency's EEO policies and programs, as outlined in its EEO program, are carried out. (15)

Suggestions for Further Research

Benchmarking can take several forms. A U.S. Department of Defense report (www.defenselink.mil/comptroller/icenter/learn/bestpracconcept.pdf) discusses four forms of benchmarking:

- *Internal benchmarking*, which studies the practices and performance within the organization itself.
- *External benchmarking*, determines the performance of others, preferably world-class organizations.
- *Quantitative benchmarking*, which allows organizations to measure progress toward goals and to set improvement objectives in terms of specific performance measures or metrics.
- *Process benchmarking*, which examines how top-performing companies accomplish a specific process. These studies are undertaken through research, surveys, interviews, and site visits.

As part of this project, the research team began identifying internal and external benchmarks. For internal benchmarking, Virginia DOT was identified as an organization that exhibited best practices. The agency met the conceptual framework in that it

- Was compliant;
- Reported its employment counts by categories that were consistent with the EEO-4 categories;
- Provided a comprehensive affirmative action report in that it not only completed an EEO-4 form but also conducted a utilization and availability analysis, as well as an analysis of the application flow; and
- Could be confident in the data it produced because it has instituted an applicant tracking system and because the DOT commissioner has effectively communicated both the importance of having a diverse workforce and his intent to hold everyone within the organization accountable for results.

In *Best Practices of Private Sector Employees* (www.eeoc.gov/abouteeoc/task_reports/prac2.html), EEOC defined a best practice as one that

- Complies with the law;
- Promotes equal employment opportunity and addresses one or more barriers that adversely affect equal employment opportunity;
- Manifests management, commitment, and accountability;
- Ensures management and employee communication;
- Produces noteworthy results; and
- Does not cause or result in unfairness.

The research team has identified the Department of Interior as an external benchmark, because it seems to have a good process for tracking progress toward achieving diversity goals and for holding people accountable for results. The performance measures included in the Department of Interior's strategic plan can be used as a guide for developing quantitative benchmarks.

The disproportionality analysis could be expanded to look at internal and external factors that affect whether there is a disproportionality between an agency's utilization and availability of women and minorities. Regression analysis could be used to determine what percentage of the disproportionality might possibly be attributed to internal and external variables.

Possible internal factors to be analyzed could include

- Total number of agency employees,
- Percentage of staff working in the EEO division,
- Total agency budget,
- Percentage of agency budget allocated to the EEO program,
- Percentage of agency budget coming from federal funds,
- Percentage of agency budget coming from local funds,
- Type of agency (public, private, public with private contractors),
- Agency leadership (commission, board, etc.),
- Number of EEO complaints,
- Number of open positions,
- Number of applicants,
- Number of new hires, and
- Number of promotions.

Possible external factors to be analyzed could include

- Total population in service area,
- Percentage of minorities (disaggregated by racial/ethnic classification),
- Percentage of women,
- Poverty rate,
- Unemployment rate,
- Percentage of population with a high school diploma (disaggregated by racial/ethnic classification),
- Percentage of population with a college degree (disaggregated by racial/ethnic classification),
- Home ownership rate,
- Density,
- Whether affirmative action ban has been proposed or passed by state legislature, and
- Political affiliation of government official (governor, mayor, county administrator).

A process benchmark would provide insight into the practices of successful agencies. The web survey developed for this project could be expanded to serve as one means of investigating best practices that could lead to the development of process benchmarks.

References

1. Lien, Marsha. Workforce Diversity: Opportunities in the Melting Pit. *Occupational Outlook Quarterly*. Vol. 48, No. 2, summer 2004, p. 28.
2. Toossi, Mitra. Employment Outlook: 2002–2012: Labor Force Projections to 2012: The Graying of the U.S. Workforce. *Monthly Labor Review,* Vol. 127, No. 2, February 2004, p. 37.
3. *The Workforce Challenge: Recruiting, Training, and Retaining Qualified Workers for Transportation and Transit Agencies.* Special Report 275. Transportation Research Board, Washington, D.C., 2003.
4. Equal Employment Opportunity Commission. Uniform Guidelines on Employee Selection Procedures. 29 C.F.R. § 1607.17, 2003.
5. Federally Assisted Programs. 42 U.S.C. § 2000d-1 et seq.
6. Equal Employment Opportunities. 42 U.S.C. § 2000e et seq.
7. Remarks of Sen. Humphrey. 110 Cong. Rec. 6548, 1964.
8. Remarks of Sen. Humphrey. 110 Cong. Rec. 6547, 1964.
9. Affirmative Action Appropriate under Title VII of the Civil Rights Act of 1964, as Amended. 29 C.F.R. § 1608.1, 2004.
10. Dale, Charles V. *Affirmative Action Revisited: A Legal History and Prospectus.* Congressional Research Service, Washington, D.C., 2004.
11. Nondiscrimination in Federally Assisted Programs of the Department of Transportation—Effectuation of Title VI of the Civil Rights Act of 1964. 49 C.F.R. § 21.1.
12. Participation by Disadvantaged Business Enterprise in Airport Concessions and Participation by Disadvantaged Business Enterprises in Department of Transportation Financial Assistance Programs. 49 C.F.R. Parts 23 and 26, 2003.
13. Dale, Charles V. *Affirmative Action in Employment: A Legal Overview.* Congressional Research Service, Washington, D.C., 2006.
14. Disadvantaged Business Enterprises: Western States Guidance for Public Transportation Providers. *Federal Register,* Vol. 71, p. 14775, Mar. 23, 2006.
15. Urban Mass Transportation Administration/U.S. Department of Transportation. Equal Opportunity Program Guidelines for Grant Recipients. Circular 4704.1. July 26, 1988.
16. Equal Employment Opportunity on Federal and Federal-Aid Construction Contracts (Including Supportive Services). 23 C.F.R. § 230.
17. EEOC Form 164: State and Local Government Information (EEO-4) Instruction Booklet. Equal Employment Opportunity Commission, Washington, D.C., 2006.
18. McGlothin Davis Inc. *Managing Transit's Workforce in the New Millennium.* TCRP Report 77. Transportation Research Board, Washington, D.C., 2002.
19. Committee on Diversity in the Engineering Workforce. *Diversity in Engineering: Managing the Workforce of the Future.* National Academy Press, Washington, D.C., 2002.
20. Public Service Human Resources Management Agency of Canada [now known as the Canada Public Service Agency]. Employment Equity in the Federal Public Service 2003–04. Annual Report to Parliament. 2005.
21. Bird, Sharon, Jacquelyn Litt, and Yong Wang. Creating Status of Women Reports: Institutional Housekeeping as 'Women's Work.' *NWSA Journal,* Vol. 16, No. 1, spring 2004, pp. 194–206.

APPENDIX A

Affirmative Action Timeline

1961

President John F. Kennedy signs Executive Order (E.O.) 10925, which instructs federal contractors to take "affirmative action" when it comes to assigning contracts. The order results in the creation of the Committee on Equal Employment Opportunity.

1964

The Civil Rights Act of 1964 was signed into law. This was landmark legislation prohibiting employment discrimination by large employers (with more than 15 employees), whether or not they have government contracts. Established the Equal Employment Opportunity Commission (EEOC).

1965

President Lyndon B. Johnson issued E.O. 11246, requiring all government contractors and subcontractors to take affirmative action to expand job opportunities for minorities. Established Office of Federal Contract Compliance (OFCC) in the Department of Labor to administer the order.

1967

President Johnson amended E.O. 11246 to include affirmative action for women. Federal contractors now required to make good-faith efforts to expand employment opportunities for women and minorities.

1970

The Labor Department, under President Richard M. Nixon, issued Order No. 4, authorizing flexible goals and timetables to correct "underutilization" of minorities by federal contractors.

1971

Order No. 4 was revised to include women. President Nixon issued E.O. 11625, directing federal agencies to develop comprehensive plans and specific program goals for a national minority Business Enterprise (MBE) contracting program.

1973

The Nixon administration issued "Memorandum-Permissible Goals and Timetables in State and Local Government employment Practices," distinguishing between proper goals and timetables and impermissible quotas.

1978

The U.S. Supreme Court in *Regents of the University of California v. Bakke*, 438 U.S. 912 (1978) upheld the use of race as one factor in choosing among qualified applicants for admission. At the same time, it also ruled unlawful the University Medical School's practice of reserving 18 seats in each entering class of 100 for disadvantaged minority students.

1979

President Jimmy Carter issued E.O. 12138, creating a National Women's Business Enterprise Policy and requiring each agency to take affirmative action to support women's business enterprises.

The Supreme Court ruled in *United Steel Workers of America, AFL-CIO v. Weber*, 444 U.S. 889 (1979) that race-conscious affirmative-action efforts designed to eliminate a conspicuous racial imbalance in an employer's workforce resulting from past discrimination are permissible if they are temporary and do not violate the rights of white employees.

1983

President Ronald Reagan issued E.O. 12432, which directed each federal agency with substantial procurement or grant-making authority to develop a Minority Business Enterprise (MBE) development plan.

1985

Efforts by some in the Reagan administration to repeal Executive Order 11246 were thwarted by defenders of affirmative action, including other Reagan administration officials, members of Congress from both parties, civil-rights organizations, and corporate leaders.

1986

The Supreme Court in *Local 128 of the Sheet Metal Workers' International Association v. EEOC*, 478 U.S. 421 (1986) upheld a judicially ordered 29 percent minority "membership admission goal" for a union that had intentionally discriminated against minorities, confirming that courts may order race-conscious relief to correct and prevent future discrimination.

1987

The Supreme Court ruled in *Johnson v. Transportation Agency, Santa Clara County, Calif.*, 480 U.S. 616 (1987) that a severe underrepresentation of women and minorities justified the use of race or sex as "one factor" in choosing among qualified candidates.

1989

The Supreme Court in *City of Richmond v. J.A. Croson Co.*, 488 U.S. 469 (1989) struck down Richmond's minority contracting program as unconstitutional, requiring that a state or local affirmative-action program be supported by a "compelling interest" and be narrowly tailored to ensure that the program furthers that interest.

1994

In *Adarand Constructors, Inc. v. Pena*, 513 U.S. 1012 (1994) the Supreme Court held that a state or local affirmative-action program remains constitutional when narrowly tailored to accomplish a compelling government interest such as remedying discrimination.

1995

President Clinton reviewed all affirmative-action guidelines by federal agencies and declared his support for affirmative-action programs by announcing the administration's policy of "mend it, don't end it."

Senator Robert Dole and Rep. Charles Canady introduced the so-called Equal Opportunity Act in Congress. The act would prohibit race or gender based affirmative action in all federal programs.

The Regents of the University of California voted to end affirmative action programs at all University of California campuses. Beginning in 1997 for graduate schools and 1998 for undergraduate admissions, officials at the University were no longer allowed to use race, gender, ethnicity or national origin as a factor in admissions decisions.

The bipartisan Glass Ceiling Commission released a report on the endurance or barriers that deny women and minorities access to decision-making positions and issued a recommendation "that corporate America use affirmative action as a tool ensuring that all qualified individuals have equal access and opportunity to compete based on ability and merit."

1996

California's Proposition 209 passed by a narrow margin in the November election. Prop. 209 abolished all public-sector affirmative action programs in the state in employment, education and contracting. Clause (C) of Prop. 209 permits gender discrimination that is "reasonably necessary" to the "normal operation" of public education, employment and contracting.

In *Texas v. Hopwood*, 518 U.S. 1033 (1996) the U.S. Court of Appeals for the Fifth Circuit ruled against the University of Texas, deciding that its law school's policy of considering race in the admissions process was a violation of the Constitution's equal-protection guarantee. The U.S. Supreme Court declined to hear an appeal of the ruling because the program at issue was no longer in use.

1997

Voters in Houston supported affirmative action programs in city contracting and hiring by rejecting an initiative that would banish such efforts. Houston proved that the wording on an initiative is a critical factor in influencing the voters' response. Instead of deceptively focusing attention on "preferential treatment," voters were asked directly if they wanted to "end affirmative action programs." They said no.

The U.S. Supreme Court refused to hear a challenge to California's Prop. 209. By declining to review the case, the court did not decide the case on its merits but allowed Prop. 209 to go into effect.

The U.S. House Judiciary Committee voted 17-9, on a bipartisan basis, to defeat legislation aimed at discriminating federal affirmative action programs for women and minorities.

Representative George Gekas (R-Pa.), who moved to table the bill, said that the bill was "useless and counterproductive. I fear that forcing the issue at this time could jeopardize the daily progress being made in ensuring equality."

Bill Lann Lee was appointed Acting Assistant Attorney General for Civil Rights after facing opposition to his confirmation because of his support for affirmative action when he worked for the NAACP Legal Defense and Educational Fund.

Lawsuits were filed against the University of Michigan and the University of Washington School of Law regarding their use of affirmative action policies in admissions standards. In response to *Hopwood*, the Texas legislature passed the Texas Ten Percent Plan, which ensures that the top ten percent of students at all high schools in Texas have guaranteed admission to the University of Texas and Texas A&M system, including the two flagships, UT-Austin and A&M-College Station.

1998

Both the United States House of Representatives and the United States Senate thwarted attempts to eliminate specific affirmative action programs. Both houses rejected amendments to abolish the Disadvantaged Business Enterprise program funded through the Transportation Bill, and the House rejected an attempt to eliminate use of affirmative action in admissions in higher education programs funded through the Higher Education Act.

Ban on use of affirmative action in admissions at the University of California went into effect. UC Berkeley had a 61 percent drop in admissions of African American, Latino/a and Native American Students, and UCLA had a 36 percent decline.

Voters in Washington passed Initiative 200 banning affirmative action in higher education, public contracting, and hiring.

2000

Many circuit courts throughout the country heard cases regarding affirmative action in higher education, including the 5th Circuit in Texas (*Hopwood*), the 6th Circuit in Michigan (*Gutter* and *Gratz*), the 9th Circuit in Washington (*Smith*), and the 11th Circuit in Georgia (*Johnson*). The same district court in Michigan made two different rulings regarding affirmative action in Michigan, with one judge deciding that the undergraduate program was constitutional while another judge found the law school program unconstitutional.

The Florida legislature passed "One Florida" Plan, banning affirmative action. The program also included the Talented 20 Percent Plan that guarantees the top 20 percent admission to the University of Florida system.

In an effort to promote equal pay, the US Department of Labor promulgated new affirmative action regulations including an Equal Opportunity Survey, which requires federal contractors to report hiring, termination, promotions, and compensation data by minority status and gender. This is the first time in history that employers have been required to report information regarding compensation by gender and minority status to the federal equal employment agencies.

The 10th Circuit issued an opinion in *Adarand Constructors v. Mineta*, 228 F.3d 1147 (10th Cir. 2000) and ruled that the Disadvantaged Business Enterprise as administered by the Department of Transportation was constitutional because it served a compelling government interest and was narrowly tailored to achieve that interest. The court also analyzed the constitutionality of the program in use when Adarand first filed suit in 1989 and determined that the previous program was unconstitutional. Adarand then petitioned the Supreme Court for a writ of certiorari.

2001

In *Adarand Constructors, Inc. v. Mineta*, 534 U.S. 103 (2001) the Supreme Court dismissed the case as "improvidently granted," thereby leaving undisturbed the 10th Circuit's decision, which upheld the government's revised federal contracting program.

California enacted a new plan allowing the top 12.5 percent of high school student's admission to the UC system, either for all four years or after two years outside the system, and guaranteeing the top 4 percent of all high school seniors' admission into the UC system.

The Sixth Circuit handed down its decision in *Gutter v. Bollinger*, 288 F.3d 732 (6th Cir. 2002) on May 14, 2002, and upheld as constitutional the use of race as one of many factors in making admissions decisions at the University of Michigan's Law School. A decision in the companion case involving the Undergraduate school at the University of Michigan, *Gratz v. Bollinger*, is imminent.

SOURCE: www.detroitnaacp.org/publicpolicy/affirmative.asp

APPENDIX B

Literature Review

Conducting a Utilization and Availability Analysis

One of the primary means for measuring whether or not an organization is achieving its goal of attaining a diverse workforce is to conduct a regular utilization and availability analysis. State DOTs and federally funded transit agencies are under a legislative mandate to complete these types of analyses as a means of monitoring their progress towards achieving this goal.

Conducting an availability and utilization analysis allows an organization to determine if there is an underutilization of a particular group and/or if a particular race or gender is being concentrated in a particular occupation. For example, according to Special Report 275, *The Workforce Challenge: Recruiting, Training, and Retaining Qualified Workers for Transportation and Transit Agencies*, "Minorities are overrepresented in bus operations as compared with information technology and engineering positions, in which Caucasian males dominate. The gender mix for bus operations is about 77 percent male and 24 percent female" (*3*). The numbers reported in *The Workforce Challenge* are aggregated because they provide the total count for minorities. It would be more useful, however, if the racial/ethnic mix for men and women were provided along with the gender concentration in bus operations.

It is important for agencies to disaggregate their employment counts by job category, each race/ethnicity, and gender when conducting an availability and utilization analysis, and not just consider the overall workforce simply by minority status or gender alone. In *The Determinants of Minority Employment in Police and Fire Departments*, O'Brien (2003) looked at the factors that affect employment of Blacks, Hispanics, Asians, and Native Americans in police and fire departments. He examined aggregated data, as well as data disaggregated by race and gender, and found that different variables, such as whether a department had an affirmative action plan or numeric goals, affected the employment rate of the different racial/ethnic groups. This study demonstrated the importance of studying both aggregated (all minorities as a group) and disaggregated (broken out by each race/ethnicity) data. The police and fire department article also used variables that were relevant to this project. In his article, the author created several key sets of variables including: geographic (whether a department was in a city or suburb); regional; population (urban and minority demographics); wage differentials; and legal (number of EEO complaints). The analysis revealed:

> There was a difference for minority groups. For police, while having just an AA policy did not increase minority employment, having both an AA policy and numeric goals did increase Black and Hispanic employment. However, having both an AA policy and numeric goals did not affect the other minority groups. For firefighters, having just an AA policy was sufficient by itself to increase Hispanic and Asian employment. However, just having an AA policy had no effect on Black and Native American employment (O'Brien 2003).

This analysis illustrates the importance of disaggregating data, because it creates more meaningful results for researchers and policy makers.

Identifying Factors that Influence Utilization Rates

There are several factors that might influence the utilization of women and minorities, but only some of which are in the control of an agency. External factors that might influence the utilization of women and minorities include local economic factors, such as a state's unemployment rate, total population, minority population, poverty rate, and the percentage of women and minorities with a high school or college degree. If there is a high unemployment rate in a particular area, then it is reasonable for a state DOT or transit agency to have low utilization rates for women and minorities. It would not be surprising for a state with a large minority population to have a larger utilization rate than a state with a small minority population.

In Jihong Zhao's (2005) article, "Predicting the Employment of Minority Officers in U.S. Cities," he states that "a substantial minority population was among the most important predictors of minority officer employment in city police departments." The percentage of women and minorities with a high school or college degree is also important because the educational level of these groups will determine what positions they are qualified to fill. The type of position available in the transit industry has changed over the past few years because the mission has shifted from one primarily focused on building roads to one that must be prepared to respond both to potential terrorist threats and to develop new transit systems. As a result, there is a growing need for additional professional positions such as planners, engineers, and IT programmers.

In addition to external factors, there are internal factors that an agency can influence. For example, agencies can create work environments hospitable to women and minorities so that they will be encouraged to apply for positions and, if hired, will stay in the industry. Gary Graham and Julie Hotchkiss (2003, 4–7) conducted research that examined which industries are most hospitable to women. Using the Current Population Survey, they developed an EEO index with five components to evaluate an agency's climate:

1. The "Equal Pay Component" measures the extent to which the employer pays women and men in the same jobs the same pay.
2. The "Occupational Segregation Component" measures the extent to which an employer's workforce is integrated, by gender, and across jobs and occupations.
3. The "Glass Ceiling Component" measures the extent to which women are represented in the upper levels of the organization.
4. The "Hiring Component" measures the extent to which women and men are proportionally represented in occupations and firms relative to their levels of availability in the relevant labor market.
5. The "Related Discrimination Component" considers the scores on the separate components from the perspective of race/ethnicity.

The authors applied this EEO index to six broad industry groups:

- Manufacturing (MAN)
- Mining and Construction (MC)
- Transportation, communication, and utilities (TCU)
- Retail and wholesale trade (TRD)
- Service (SRV)
- Finance, insurance, and real estate (FIN).

The two industries relevant to state DOTs and transit agencies are mining and construction (MC) and transportation, communication, and utilities (TCU). According to the authors' analysis, "both MC and TCU have indexes below the market norm. MC's poor index was driven by its significantly below average performance on three out of five components." It scored below the norm on: Occupational Segregation, Glass Ceiling, and Related Discrimination.

Graham and Hotchkiss argue that organizations "operating in poorly-performing industries might be slated for greater enforcement efforts by agencies such as Equal Employment Opportunity Commission (EEOC) and Office of Federal Contract Compliance Programs (OFCCP)." They further note that the EEOC does not systematically evaluate the staffing data it collects through the EEO reports and recommend that the EEOC and other agencies that monitor EEO performance have a more routine assessment of industry performance on EEO efforts.

Effective leadership is another key internal factor that can influence an agency's success in fully utilizing women and minorities. Leadership needs to communicate the importance of diversity in the organization. This communication can be in the form of formal written statements, as well as through regular company-wide correspondence meetings, and other communication tools. In its report, *Best Practices of Private Sector Employers*, the EEOC states:

> Management must have a positive and unequivocal commitment to equal employment opportunity. Without commitment from top-level management to front-line supervisors, nothing can reasonably be expected to be done. Management commitment must be a driving force.... Management should participate and interact with employees and employee groups. It should encourage ongoing discussions about diversity issues. Communication should be encouraged from "top-down" and "bottom-up", including CEO speeches to employees and letters from employee to management. (EEOC 1997)

Jeffrey Gandz (2001), in *A Business Case for Diversity*, also discusses the importance of leadership. He says, "One critical requirement in achieving diversity is a clear, unequivocal statement by organizational leaders of the importance of doing so." In addition to having a clear statement, Gandz emphasizes the importance of "walking the talk," which means making sure these statements are followed up with concrete actions. Finally, Layne (2002) also discusses leadership in *Best Practices in Managing Diversity, Leadership and Management in Engineering*. It is not enough to have mid and lower level employees committed to diversity; management must also be involved. "The chief executive officer, senior management, and the board of directors of the organization must demonstrate their commitment to workforce diversity. This must be done not only by issuing statements and developing policies, but also by making decisions and taking actions that reflect that commitment" (Layne 2002).

Benchmarking Best Practices

One of this project's main goals is the development of benchmarks to measure racial and gender diversity in state DOTs and transit agencies. The first step then is to define the term "benchmark." A benchmark has been defined as:

1. A systematic and continuous process to *identify, determine, measure, compare, learn, adopt and implement* the best practices obtained through internal and external evaluation of an organization so that performance of a higher standard can be achieved and improved. [emphasis added] (Endut et al., 2000)
2. A standard of performance … [which] allows organizations to discover *where they stand in relation to others* [emphasis added] (U. S. Department of Defense date unknown).

Before establishing a benchmark, one should identify what type of benchmark they want to establish. In *Best Practices & Benchmarking: Making Worthwhile Comparisons* (U. S. Department of Defense date unknown), four forms of benchmarking are discussed:

1. **Internal benchmarking** studies the practices and performance within the organization itself.
2. **External benchmarking** determines the performance of others, preferably world-class companies.
3. **Quantitative benchmarking** allows organizations to measure progress toward goals and to set improvement objectives in terms of specific performance measures or metrics.
4. **Process benchmarking** examines how top performing companies accomplish a specific process. These studies are undertaken through research, surveys, interviews, and site visits.

Also discussed in *Best Practices & Benchmarking: Making Worthwhile Comparisons* is how an organization can conduct a "gap analysis," which is a "method that helps identify the performance or operational differences between your process and that of your benchmarking partners, and why the differences are there." A gap analysis involves taking a look at how things are and comparing them to how you want them to be.

In our review of the Transportation Research Board's current research projects, we found other benchmarking studies that are currently in progress. One of the objectives of *Benchmarking for North Carolina Public Transportation Systems* (TRB 2004) is to develop a set of "efficiency and effectiveness benchmarks that are commonly used by other transit systems." The researcher of the North Carolina project defines benchmarking as "a process to establish standards, targets and/or best practices in regard to performance measurement."

In another TRB sponsored benchmarking project, *Analysis and Benchmarking of State DOT Recruitment and Hiring Practices* (TRB 2005), the researchers plan to "analyze and benchmark HR best practices for recruiting and hiring transportation agency employees at entry and mid-career levels." According to the project overview, "There currently exists little information and no mechanism for comparison of human resource (HR) best practice benchmarks of state departments of transportation (DOTs) and other transportation agencies." This recruitment and hiring study will survey practices of state DOTs, other governmental agencies, and private and nonprofit organizations to develop a list of best practices. After the initial list of best practices has been developed, the researchers plan to refine the list based on the outcome of site visits and telephone interviews. The best practices will be organized within defined peer categories, which will be based on demographics and organizational structure.

In *Managing Transit's Workforce in the New Millennium*, the authors developed benchmarks for key positions in the transit industry. A telephone benchmarking survey was administered to 50 HR managers or transit managers in small, medium, and large transit agencies. The purpose of the survey was to "determine the positions most difficult to recruit for and to retain employees in." The researchers received data from 33 of the 50 agencies, a 66% response rate. From these responses, the team developed a tentative list of benchmark positions. According to the report, "bus operators and mechanics were mentioned most often as difficult to recruit and retain followed by information technology professionals, engineers, and customer relations representatives." The researchers then developed a survey, which they mailed to 200 small, medium, and large transit agencies. "The purpose of the survey was to understand how transit agencies recruit, train and retain employees in the benchmark positions." Of the 200 surveys, 53 were completed, resulting in a 27% response rate. The researchers used the results of the survey to develop a list of 15 agencies to visit in order to prepare case studies. The agencies were grouped by size and were representative of different geographic regions. One of the goals of the study was to develop a core skill set for the benchmark positions. The researchers were able to identify a set of skills for transit mechanics, but were not able to identify a detailed skill set for the other benchmark positions.

Developing Benchmarks

Developing a benchmark requires extensive research and data collection. The Government Accounting Office (GAO) outlines a series of steps to develop a benchmark. It instructs organizations to

1. Understand the government process [they] want to improve,
2. Research to plan the review,
3. Select appropriate organizations,
4. Collect data from selected organizations,
5. Identify barriers to change, and
6. Make recommendations for change constructive and convincing. (U. S. Department of Defense, Date Unknown)

In order to understand the government process, GAO suggests that organizations discuss the process with agency officials and then illustrate it in a flowchart. Implementing this suggestion would help understand how state DOTs and transit agencies develop and measure their diversity and affirmative action goals.

From our review of the data, it appears that there is no uniform way to collect and report the utilization and availability rates for women and minority employees. There were, however, some agencies that seemed to have a good process in place. The GAO recommends that when selecting appropriate organizations for the comparison group, the organization looking for comparisons should find companies that experts consider among the best at the process being reviewed.

In the benchmarking process, there are numerous options for selecting a comparison group. In *Benchmarking for North Carolina Public Transportation Systems* (TRB 2004) the authors state that comparisons can be made with (1) some kind of industry standards, (2) appropriate organizational goals or targets, (3) the performance of a peer group, or (4) the "best practices" of other similar organizations. In *Best Practices in Managing Diversity, Leadership and Management in Engineering* (Layne 2002), the author discusses best practices to manage diversity in the engineering industry. According to the author, "benchmarking against results in other organizations" is a key component of a successful diversity program, and "successful companies keep track of what their competition is doing in the area of diversity, just as they do with other business goals."

In *A Business Case for Diversity*, Jeffrey Gandz (2001) argues that it is a mistake to search only within one's own industry. He believes that "Just looking at one's direct competitors is a myopic view of the benchmarking process. Learning from the best, about the best practices, and about the things that work and the things that should be avoided is critically important if many of the pitfalls of diversity management are to be avoided."

The best practices of a select group of private and public sector organizations are discussed in the Best Practices section of this report (Appendix E).

The complete list of references consulted for this literature review is provided in the Bibliography (Appendix C).

APPENDIX C
Bibliography

Bird, Sharon, Jacquelyn Litt, and Yong Wang. "Creating Status of Women Reports: Institutional Housekeeping as "Women's Work." *NWSA Journal,* Vol. 16, No. 1 (Spring 2004) pp. 194–206.

Bureau of Labor Statistics, U.S. Department of Labor. "Workforce Diversity: Opportunities in the Melting Pit" by Marsha Lien. *Occupational Outlook Quarterly*, Vol. 48, No. 2 (Summer 2004) p. 28.

Bureau of Labor Statistics, U.S. Department of Labor. "Employment Outlook: 2002–12: Labor Force Projections to 2012: The Graying of the U.S. Workforce" by Mitra Toossi. *Monthly Labor Review*, Vol. 127, No. 2 (February 2004) p. 37.

Burke, Jake and William L. Kuechler. "Web-Based Surveys for Corporate Information Gathering: A Bias-Reducing Design Framework." *IEEE Transactions on Professional Communication,* Vol. 46, No. 2 (June 2003) p. 81.

Celec, Stephen E., et al. "Measuring Disparity in Government Procurement: Problems with Using Census Data in Estimating Availability." *Public Administration Review*, Vol. 60, No. 2 (2000) p. 134.

Coleman, Major G. "Contesting the Magic of the Market-place: Black Employment and Business Concentration in the Urban Context." *Urban Studies,* Vol. 39, No. 10 (September 2002) pp. 1793–1818.

Coombes, Mike and Jim Hubbuck. "Monitoring Equal Employment Opportunity at the Workplace: The Crucial Role of the United Kingdom 1991 Census." *Ethnic and Racial Studies,* Vol. 15, No. 2 (April 1992) pp. 93–213.

Curry, Sheree R. "Little Progress Seen in Diversity." *Television Week*, Vol. 24, No. 31 (August 2005) pp. 11–13.

Endut, Wan Wan Jaafar, Mokhtar Abdullah, and Nooreha Husain. "Benchmarking Institutions of Higher Education." *Total Quality Management*, Vol. 11, Nos. 4/5/6 (Jul 2000).

Gandz, Jeffrey. "A Business Case for Diversity." Richard Ivey School of Business. (2001), www.sdc.gc.ca/en/lp/lo/lswe/we/special_projects/RacismFreeInitiative/BusinessCase.pdf

Georgetown University Department of Psychology. "Research Methods and Statistics Resources," www.georgetown.edu/departments/psychology/researchmethods/researchanddesign/validityandreliability.htm

Government Accounting Office. "*Equal Employment Opportunity: Women and Minority Aerospace Managers and Professionals, 1979–86.*" Government Accounting Office, Washington, D.C. (1989). http://archive.gao.gov/d26t7/139889.pdf

Graham, Mary E. and Julie Hotchkiss. "Which Industries Are the Best Employers for Women? An Application of a New Equal Employment Opportunity Index." Federal Reserve Bank of Atlanta, Working Paper 2003–11 (July 2003).

Guajardo, S. A. "Minority Employment in US Federal Agencies: Continuity and Change." *Public Personnel Management,* Vol. 25, No. 2 (1996) pp. 199–208.

Holzer, Harry J. and Jens Ludwig. "Measuring Discrimination in Education: Are Methodologies from Labor and Markets Useful? *Teachers College Record,* Vol. 105, No. 6 (August 2003) pp. 1147–1178.

Layne, Peggy E. "Best Practices in Managing Diversity, Leadership and Management in Engineering." Vol. 2, No. 4 (October 2002) pp. 28–30.

Martin, Clark. "Help Wanted—Meeting the Need for Tomorrow's Transportation Work Force." *Public Roads,* Vol. 65, No. 1 (July/August 2001). www.tfhrc.gov/pubrds/julaug01/helpwanted.htm

McCall, Jean. "Managing Diversity: One Firm's Perspective." *Leadership and Management in Engineering,* Vol. 2, No. 4 (October 2002) pp. 31–33. http://link.aip.org/getpdf/servlet/GetPDFServlet?filetype=pdf&id=LMEEAZ000002000004000031000001&idtype=cvips&prog=normal

McGill, Lawrence T. "*Newsroom Diversity: Meeting the Challenge.*" The Freedom Forum Board of Trustees, Arlington, VA. www.freedomforum.org/publications/diversity/meetingthechallenge/meetingthechallenge.pdf

McGlothin Davis, Inc.—"*TCRP Report 77: Managing Transit's Workforce in the New Millennium.*" TRB, National Research Council, Washington, D.C. (2002). trb.org/publications/Publications.asp

McInnes, R. Workforce Diversity: Changing the Way You Do Business. Diversity World, Focus, Workforce Diversity (IBM), (1999). www.diversityworld.com/Diversity/workforce_diversity.htm

Meeting of November 16, 2005, Washington, D.C. on Operations in Wake of Hurricane Katrina and Revisions to EEO-1 Report. www.eeoc.gov/abouteeoc/meetings/11-16-05/

Milam, Jr., John H. "The Myth of Affirmative Action Data." Paper presented at the Annual Forum of the Association for Institutional Research, Boston (1995).

———. *National Study of Faculty Availability and Utilization: Report of the Findings.* HigherEd. Org Inc., Winchester, VA. (1996). highered.org/docs/milam-facultyavailability.PDF

National Academy of Engineering. Committee on Diversity in the Engineering Workforce. *Diversity in Engineering: Managing the Workforce of the Future* (2002).

National Highway Traffic Safety Administration. "Equal Employment Opportunities and Affirmative Employment for Minorities, Women, and People with Disabilities Accomplishment Report and Updates, Fiscal Year 1998." National Highway Traffic Safety Administration, Washington, D.C. (1999).

Newgarden, Peggy. "Establishing Affirmative Action Goals for Women." *Public Administration Review,* Vol. 36, No. 4 (Jul.–Aug. 1976).

O'Brien, Kevin M. "The Determinants of Minority Employment in Police and Fire Departments." *Journal of Socio-Economics,* Vol. 32, No. 2 (May 2003) pp. 183–195.

Patten, Mildred L. *Understanding Research Methods: An Overview of the Essentials* 3rd ed. Pyrczak Publishing, Los Angeles, CA (2002).

Potts, Lee W. "Equal Employment Opportunity and Female Employment in Police Agencies." *Journal of Criminal Justice,* Vol. 11, No. 6 (1983) pp. 505–523.

Potts, Lee W. "Equal Employment Opportunity and Female Criminal Justice Employment." *Police Studies,* Vol. 4, No. 3 (1981) pp. 9–19.

Price, Vivian. "Race, Affirmative Action, and Women's Employment in US Highway Construction." *Feminist Economics,* Vol. 8, No. 2 (2002) pp. 87–113.

Public Service Human Resources Management Agency of Canada. *Employment Equity in the Federal Public Service 2003–2004.* (2005). www.hrma-agrh.gc.ca/reports-rapports/dwnld/EE03-04_e.pdf

Schutt, Russell K. *Investigating the Social World: The Process and Practice of Research* 2nd ed. Pine Forge Press, Thousand Oaks (1999).

Solso, Robert L., Homer H. Johnson, and M. Kimberly Beal. *Experimental Psychology: A Case Approach* 6th ed. Longman, New York (1998).

Spokane County Equal Employment Opportunity Plan, July 1, 2002–June 30, 2004. www.spokanecounty.org/hr/pdf/eeo_plan.pdf

Subcommittee on Oversight of Government Management, Restructuring, and the District of Columbia. "Report to the President: The Crisis in Human Capital." Prepared by Senator George V. Voinovich. (December 2000). voinovich.senate.gov/humancapital.pdf

Terkkonen, L. and L. Vehkalahti. "Measurement Errors in Multivariate Measurement Scales." *Journal of Multivariate Analysis,* Vol. 96, No. 1 (2005) pp. 172–189.

TRB. *Management of Disadvantaged Business Enterprise Issues in Construction Contracting, A Synthesis of Highway Practice. NCHRP Synthesis 343.* TRB, National Research Council, Washington, D.C. (2005). trb.org/publications/nchrp/nchrp_syn_343.pdf

TRB. *Benchmarking for North Carolina Public Transportation Systems.* (2004). rip.trb.org/browse/dproject.asp?n=10014 or www.ncdot.org/doh/preconstruct/tpb/research/2005-12.html

TRB. *Diversity Training Initiatives: A Synthesis of Transit Practice.* TCRP Synthesis 46. TRB, National Research Council, Washington, D.C. (2003a). gulliver.trb.org/publications/tcrp/tcrp_syn_46a.pdf

TRB. *The Workforce Challenge: Recruiting, Training, and Retaining Qualified Workers for Transportation and Transit Agencies.* TRB, National Research Council, Washington, D.C. (2003b).

TRB. *Managing Transit's Workforce in the New Millennium.* TRB, National Research Council, Washington, D.C. (2002). http://trb.org/publications/tcrp/tcrp_rpt_77.pdf

TRB. Research in Progress. *Analysis and Benchmarking of State DOT Recruitment and Hiring Practices. National Cooperative Highway Research Program Project 20–24(40).* TRB, National Research Council, Washington, D.C. (2005). http://www4.trb.org/trb/crp.nsf/All+Projects/NCHRP+20-24(40)

TRB. Research in Progress. *Benchmarking for North Carolina Public Transportation Systems.* TRB, National Research Council, Washington, D.C. rip.trb.org/browse/dproject.asp?n=10014

TRB. Research in Progress. *Benchmarking Public Involvement.* TRB, National Research Council, Washington, D.C. rip.trb. org/browse/orgprj.asp?i=660&n=Program+for+Community+Problem+Solving+(National+Civic+League)

TRB. *Developing Transportation Agency Leaders: A Synthesis of Highway Practice.* National Cooperative Highway Research Program. Synthesis 349. Research Sponsored by the American Association of State Highway and Transportation Officials in Cooperation with the Federal Highway Administration. TRB, National Research Council, Washington, D.C. trb.org/publications/nchrp/nchrp_syn_349.pdf

TRB. *Managing Change in State Department of Transportation.* NCHRP Web Document 39 (Project SP20-24[14]): Contractor's Final Report. TRB, National Research Council, Washington, D.C. gulliver.trb.org/publications/nchrp/nchrp_w39-1.pdf

Trends and Issues in Transportation—TRB's 1997 Field Visit Program. *TR News 194,* Jan.–Feb. (1998) pp. 37–55. gulliver.trb.org/publications/trnews/field2.html

Truesdell, William H. *Get Ready to Count Race & Ethnicity to Match New EEO-1 Report.* The Management Advantage, Inc. (2005). www.management-advantage.com/products/NewEEO-1Categories.htm

UMTA. *Equal Employment Opportunity Program Guidelines for Grant Recipients.* (UMTA C 4704.1), Urban Mass Transportation Administration, Office of Civil Rights. (1988).

U. S. Department of Defense. OSD Comptroller ID Center. *Best Practices & Benchmarking: Making Worthwhile Comparisons.* (Date Unknown). www.dod.mil/comptroller/icenter/learn/bestpracconcept.pdf

U.S. Department of the Interior. *Strategic Plan for Achieving and Maintaining a Highly Skilled and Diverse Workforce, FY 2005–2009.* (February 17, 2005). www.r6.fws.gov/dcr/Strategic%20Plan.pdf

U.S. Department of Transportation. *Federal Transit Administration: FY06 Strategic Business Plan.* (2005). www.fta.dot.gov/documents/SBP__Final_FY06_Deliverables_11-15-051.pdf

U.S. Department of Transportation. *Performance and Accountability for FY 2005.* (2005). www.dot.gov/perfacc2005/pdf/entirepar2005.pdf

U.S. Department of Transportation Federal Highway Administration. *Innovative Practices in State DOT Workforce Management, Employee Retention: Benchmarking Hiring Process Saves Time and Employees* (date unknown). www.nhi.fhwa.dot.gov/transworkforce/IP_NH.PDF

U. S. Equal Employment Opportunity Commission. *Best Practices of Private Sector Employers.* (1997). www.eeoc.gov/abouteeoc/task_reports/practice.html

U.S. Equal Employment Opportunity Commission. *Census 2000 Special EEO File Questions & Answers.* www.eeoc.gov/stats/census/qanda.html

U.S. Equal Employment Opportunity Commission. *Job Patterns for Minorities and Women in Private Industry: A Glossary.* www.eeoc.gov/stats/jobpat/glossary.html

U.S. Equal Employment Opportunity Commission. *Questions & Answers: Revisions to the EEO-1 Report.* (2005). www.eeoc.gov/eeo1/qanda.html

United States Office of Personnel Management. *Federal Equal Opportunity Recruitment Program, Annual Report to Congress, FY 2004.* (May 2005).

United States Office of Personal Management. *Building and Maintaining a Diverse and High Quality Workforce: A Guide for Federal Agencies.* Employment Service Diversity Office. (June 25, 2000).

Zhao, Jihong. "Predicting the Employment of Minority Officers in U.S. Cities: OLS Fixed-effect Panel Model Results for African American and Latino Officers for 1993, 1996, and 2000." *Journal of Criminal Justice,* Vol. 33, No. 4 (July 2005).

APPENDIX D

Survey Findings

General Findings

The initial universe for the web survey was 52 state agencies. Five were invited to participate in the pretest and 47 were targeted for the final web survey. However, some state transportation departments had recently changed their web pages and email addresses. Despite extensive efforts, we could not obtain correct email addresses for seven agencies in time to include them in the survey. In addition, one potential respondent answered our email by notifying us that he/she preferred not to answer a web survey. Thus, our universe for the finalized survey was reduced to 39 agencies. Twenty-nine of the 39 agencies responded to our survey, leading to a 74% response rate.

In six cases (21%), a person other than the person to whom the email was originally sent answered the survey. It appears that these respondents worked in the offices in charge of racial and gender diversity issues, but these respondents did not have enough knowledge about the frequency of data collection, job classification targets, or utilization and availability data, needed to process and complete EEO forms.

In only in one case did both the EEO officer and the EEO director answer the entire questionnaire. When we present the analysis on a case by case basis, we will discuss the consistency of both responses and the real knowledge that some directors could have about the topic.

Analysis by Variables

Equal Employment Opportunity Reporting

Our entire sample answered that they collect information on the number of women and minorities employed at their agencies. However, only 62% of respondents were responsible for collecting this information for their respective agencies.

How often does your agency collect this information?

	Frequency	%
Weekly	3	11.11
Biweekly	1	3.70
Monthly	9	33.33
Quarterly	5	18.52
Semi-annually	1	3.70
Annually	3	11.11
Other	5	18.52
Total	27	100.00

How often does your agency update this information?

	Frequency	%
Weekly	3	11.11
Biweekly	2	7.41
Monthly	10	37.04
Quarterly	5	18.52
Semi-annually	1	3.70
Annually	3	11.11
Other	3	11.11
Total	27	100.00

When asked about specific policies for hiring women, 89% of the respondents declared that their agencies have goals or targets for the percentage of women it seeks to employ. However, only 72% stated that these goals or targets were for a particular job classification. When analyzing job classifications, we found that more than 67% of the state transportation agencies that have targets for particular job classifications have a clear policy of hiring women in high skill jobs (officials and managers, 67%; professionals, 72%; and technicians, 78%). For mid-skill laborers it seems that there are few clear policies for hiring women (sales workers, 5%; and administrative support workers, 44%). But when we examine low-skill laborers, more than 44% of the agencies have goals for hiring women (craft workers, 61%; operatives, 44%; laborers and helpers, 61%; and service workers, 56%).

When asked about specific policies for minority hiring, 78% of the respondents declared that their agencies have goals or targets for the percentage of minorities it seeks to employ. However, only 67% of them stated that these goals or targets were for a particular job classification. When analyzing job classifications, we found that more than 71% of the state transportation agencies that have targets for particular job classifications have a clear policy of hiring minorities in high skill jobs (officials and managers, 72%; professionals, 86%; and technicians, 86%). For mid-skill laborers it seems that there are few clear policies to hire women (sales workers, 14%; and administrative support workers, 50%). Finally, when we consider low skill laborers, there are different policies for different job categories (craft workers, 71%; operatives, 36%; laborers and helpers, 64%; and service workers, 50%).

It appears that the information that state transportation agencies have on minorities is accurate because 89% of the respondents stated that employees self report their minority and/or ethnic classification.

The most frequent classification for reporting minority/ethnic identity used by state agencies is a classification similar to the Census, but it includes Hispanic as a separate category.

Does your agency use the following minority/ethnic classification?

	Frequency	%
Census classification	5	23.81
Office of Management and Budget classification	2	9.52
Other classification (includes Hispanic)	14	66.67
Total	21	100.00

The percentage of respondents who are responsible for reporting data is higher than the percentage of respondents who are responsible for collecting data, 74% vs. 62%. This means that even when the respondents are not the ones who collect or supervise the collection of data directly, almost all of them are in charge of reporting this data, given their position in their agencies.

Availability

It is important to note that 15% of the agencies do not collect data about the availability of employees by race and/or ethnicity in their geographic market. Without this information, even if they have targets on minority issues, they are not going to be able to provide an adequate solution due to lack of information.

How does your agency collect availability data?

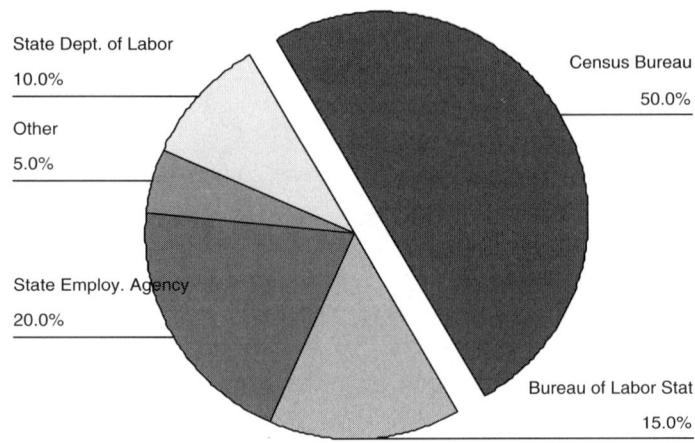

Utilization

Twenty agencies answered the question: "Does your agency complete a government EEO form?" Twenty percent of the agencies that responded to this question indicated that they do not complete these forms, while 80% answered that they did. Of these 20 agencies, eight complete Form 164 (EEO-4); eight agencies complete FHWA-1392, and six agencies complete other forms. Some of these agencies complete more than one form.

All of these 20 respondents answered that their agencies prepared an affirmative action plan. However, the frequency shows that different state agencies renew these plans on different schedules. Sixty-five percent update it annually. Other states make substantial changes after each Census, while 15% update their plans as needed and 10% update biannually or more frequently. Five percent update monthly and another 5% quarterly.

Perceptions

Not all of the respondents are extremely confident in the accuracy of their agencies EEO reports. Fifty-eight percent are extremely confident and 42 percent are somewhat confident. When they compare their reporting process to the reporting processes of other transportation agencies, 26 percent think that they perform better and 74 percent think that they perform similarly to other agencies.

Directors of human rights in state departments of transportation perceive that there is a disparity between the percentages of available female and minority employees qualified to work in their agencies and the current percentage of females and minorities employed by their agencies. Fifty-nine percent of the respondents answered that they believe that there is a disparity in the case of females, whereas 68% believe that there is disparity in the case of minorities.

Do you think there is a disparity between the percentage of available female employees qualified to work in your agency and the current percentage of females employed by your agency?

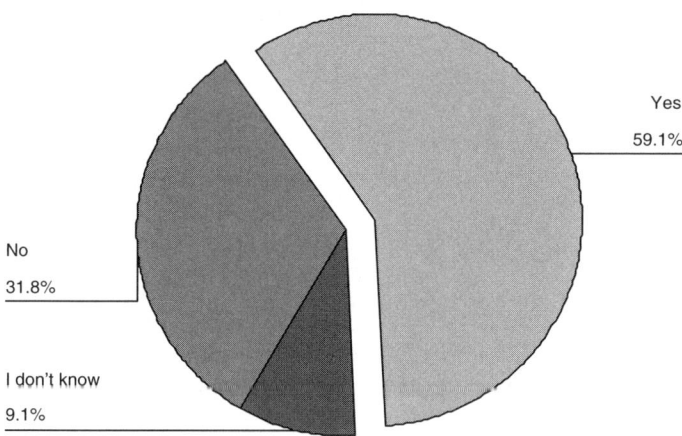

Do you think there is a disparity between the percentage of available minority employees qualified to work in your agency and the current percentage of minorities employed by your agency?

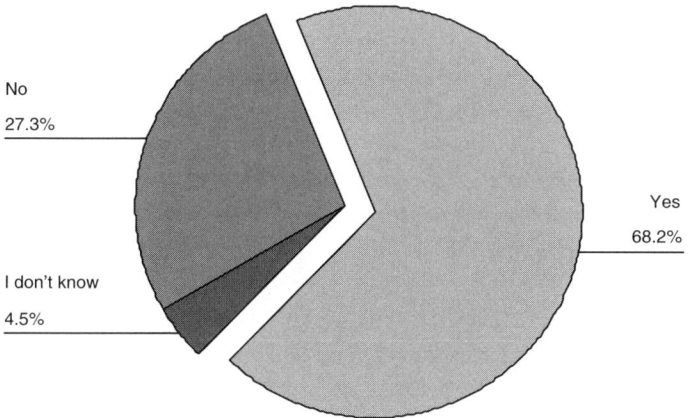

Eighty-four percent of the respondents state that they communicate with people in other state or federal agencies who do work similar to theirs, and 63% answered that they have attended an affirmative action training seminar. Eighty-four percent believe that their agency's EEO reporting processes could be improved. This result shows that training and communication are not enough to improve EEO reporting processes. Some respondents stated that they need more compromise from their agencies, better training, clearer guidelines, and more specific requirements for EEO reports. Their direct comments included the following:

- There should be greater awareness on Human Resource's personnel (in which we rely for data) of the importance of timely and accurate submission of data. However, despite efforts, this requires a change in mentality, which is not easily achieved.

- The data that are available could be used more by the top managers to help eliminate court cases and solve daily managerial decisions.
- Having clear guidelines of what should be reported and how to establish required goals.
- Being more precise with our data and where and how we get that data.
- Reduction in the amount of information that is reported.
- We need better resources, a better computing system, and equipment. We need better training on making the reports more accurate. We need to benchmark against best practices of those agencies that do a good job. The reports have to be used and be given the priority of constant analysis.
- There could be more requirements for biannual reviews of EEO updates. The state requires an annual plan, but does not provide more specific training about affirmative action planning or action-oriented goals to strive for on a bi-annual or quarterly basis.
- Report more frequently.

Some of the respondents also reported a lack of time or resources to accomplish this task, suggesting that the agency ought "to hire someone else to do the job" or "uncertainty" about what to do.

Others expressed enthusiasm for this task:

- Think any process can be improved. No process is perfect. Always be looking for new ideas and innovative ways to evaluate the department's affirmative action plan.
- It's constantly changing. As improvements are detected or noted, action is taken.

Case Analysis

One third of the respondents answered that they were not the person responsible for collecting information on the number of women and minorities employed by their agency. Half of these respondents, however, exited the survey after responding to only a few questions. This may be because they felt the survey was completely related to these topics.

The following paragraphs show how respondent characteristics could affect their responses. We controlled for education and the amount of time one worked for a transportation agency. In addition, we looked into the behavior of states that do not complete any forms by exploring their responses on data availability, utilization, and their comprehension of equal employment opportunity.

Education

When controlling for education, results show that people with high school diplomas have different perceptions about availability and utilization issues, as well as on EEO reports than do respondents with other levels of education.

For example, in response to the question, "Do you think there is a disparity between the percentage of available female employees qualified to work in your agency and the current percentage of females employed by your agency?" all respondents with a high school education answered "no," whereas just 33% of respondents with some college education, 40% with a college degree, 0% with some graduate school, and 38% with a graduate degree answered "no" to the same question.

Similarly, to the question, "Do you think there is a disparity between the percentage of available minority employees qualified to work in your agency and the current percentage of minorities employed by your agency?" all respondents with a high school diploma answered "no," whereas 33% of respondents with some college education, 40% with a college degree, 0% with some graduate school, and 25% with a graduate degree answered "no" to the same question.

In the same vein, to the question, "How confident are you in the accuracy of your agency's EEO reports?" all respondents with a high school education answered "somewhat confident," whereas 0% of respondents with some college education, 60% with a college education, 50% with some graduate school, and 38% with a graduate degree answered "somewhat confident" to the same question.

Likewise, to the question, "Do you think your agency's EEO reporting process could be improved?" all respondents with a high school diploma answered "no," whereas 0% of respondents with some college education, 40% with a college degree, and 0% for both those with some graduate school and with a graduate degree answered "no" to the same question. Answers to these questions are interesting because it seems that respondents with more education believe that the process can be improved, while those with a high school education do not.

States That Do Not Complete Any Forms

With respect to equal employment opportunity reporting, 75% of the respondents were responsible for collecting information on the number of women and minorities employed at their agencies and 25% were not. These agencies update their information frequently: 25% weekly, 50% monthly, and 25% quarterly.

When asked about specific policies for hiring women, 75% of the respondents declared that their agencies have goals or targets for the percentage of women they seek to employ. However, only 50% of them stated that these goals or targets were for a particular job classification. When analyzing job classifications, we found that more than 50% of the state transportation agencies that have targets for particular job classifications have clear policies for hiring women in high-skill jobs (officials and managers, 50%; professionals, 100%; and technicians, 100%). For mid-skill laborers it seems that the agencies do not have clear policies for hiring women (sales workers, 0%; and administrative support workers, 50%). But when we review the numbers on low skill-laborers more than 50% of the agencies have goals for hiring women, except for operatives (craft workers, 100%; operatives, 0%; laborers and helpers, 50%; and service workers, 100%).

When asking about specific policies for minority hiring, 50% of the respondents declared that their agencies have goals or targets for the percentage of minorities it seeks to employ. The same percentage stated that these goals or targets were for particular job classifications. When we analyzed job classifications, we found that more than 50% of the state transportation agencies that have targets for particular job classifications have clear policies for hiring minorities in high-skill jobs (officials and managers, 50%; professionals, 100%; and technicians, 100%). For mid-skill laborers, it seems that agencies do not have clear policies for hiring minorities (sales workers, 0%; and administrative support workers, 50%). Finally, when we examine low-skill laborers, there are different policies based on job categories (craft workers, 100%; operatives, 0%; laborers and helpers, 50%; and service workers, 100%).

It looks like the information on minority hiring that state transportation agencies have is correct since 100% of the respondents stated that employees self report their minority and/or ethnic classification.

The most frequent classification for reporting minority/ethnic identity used by state agencies is a classification similar to the Census, but it includes Hispanic as a separate category.

The percentage of respondents who are responsible for reporting data is higher than the percentage of the respondents who are responsible for collecting data, 100% vs. 75%. This means that even when the respondents are not the people who collect or supervise the collection of data directly, all of them are in charge of reporting this data, given their positions in their agencies.

It is important to note that all these agencies collect data about the availability of employees by race and/or ethnicity in their geographic market.

All of the respondents answered that their agencies prepare affirmative action plans. However, the frequency shows us that different state agencies renew these plans on different schedules. Twenty-five percent update their plans quarterly, and 75% do so annually.

Directors of human rights at state departments of transportation that do not complete any EEO form do not perceive a disparity between the percentage of available female employees qualified to work in their agencies and the percentage of females currently employed by their agencies. Zero percent responded that they believe that there is a disparity in the case of females, whereas 33% believe that there is disparity in the case of minorities employed. This result is interesting, because in the overall sample, more than half of the interviewees believed that there were disparities for both females and minorities.

Do you think there is a disparity between the percentage of available female employees qualified to work in your agency and the current percentage of females employed by your agency?

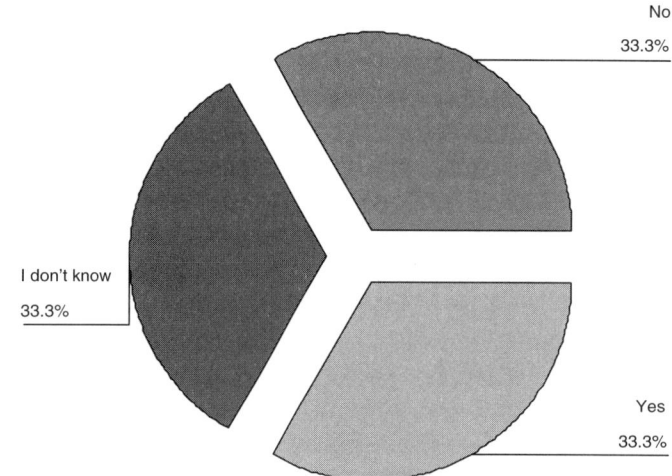

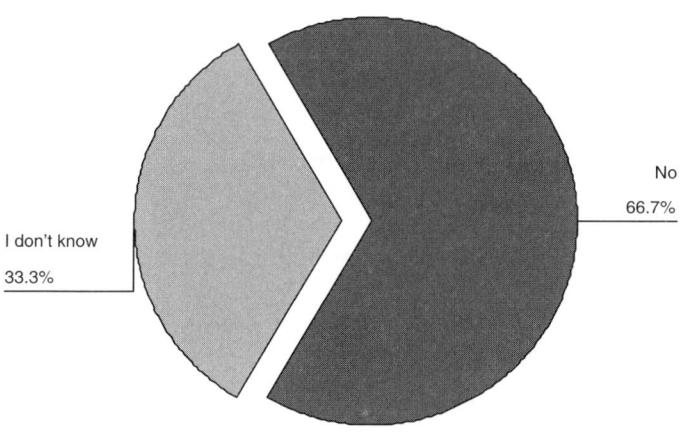

Do you think there is a disparity between the percentage of available minority employees qualified to work in your agency and the current percentage of minorities employed by your agency?

All the respondents are confident in the accuracy of their agency's EEO reports; 50% are extremely confident and 50% are somewhat confident. When they compare their reporting processes to the reporting processes of other transportation agencies, 100% think that they perform similarly, which differs from the overall sample where 25% believed that they performed better.

Summary

Respondents in the survey who provided EEO reports were not uniformly confident (responding that they were "extremely confident") that the data they provided was accurate. A sizeable minority of the respondents indicated that they themselves were not the ones responsible for data collection. Although many reported that there was a disparity between availability and utilization of women and minorities, there were many differences across agencies in how racial or ethnic categories were defined. Respondents confirmed what was found in the administrative data review: that availability and utilization data were not universally collected by state departments of transportation.

APPENDIX E

Best Practices

The EEOC prepared a report, *Best Practices of Private Sector Employers* (EEOC 1997), which summarizes the best practices of numerous private sector employers in terms of recruitment and hiring, promotion and career advancement, terms and conditions of employment, termination and downsizing, alternative dispute resolution, policies and programs as well as management commitment and accountability. The report defines a best practice as one that

- Complies with the law;
- Promotes equal employment opportunity and addresses one or more barriers that adversely affect equal employment opportunity;
- Manifests management commitment and accountability;
- Ensures management and employee communication;
- Produces noteworthy results; and
- Does not cause or result in unfairness. (EEOC 1997)

In addition to defining a best practice, the report also presents a conceptual framework based on the approaches taken by the organizations that were identified as having the best practices. The organizations highlighted in the report (EEOC 1997) are said to have used the "SPLENDID" Approach, which stands for STUDY, PLAN, LEAD, ENCOURAGE, NOTICE, DISCUSSION, INCLUSION, and DEDICATION.

The "Splendid" Approach (EEOC 1997)

STUDY Since one cannot solve problems that one doesn't know exists, know the law, the standards that define one's obligations, and the various barriers to EEO and diversity. Assistance can be obtained from EEOC, professional consultants, associations or groups, etc.

PLAN Know one's own circumstances (workforce and demographics—locally, nationally, and globally). Define one's problem(s), propose solutions, and develop strategies for achieving them.

LEAD Senior, middle, and lower management must champion the cause of diversity as a business imperative, and provide leadership for successful attainment of the vision of a diverse workforce at all levels of management.

ENCOURAGE Companies should encourage the attainment of diversity by all managers, supervisors, and employees, and structure their business practices and reward systems to reinforce those corporate objectives. Link pay and performance not only for technical competencies, but also for how employees interact, support, and respect each other.

NOTICE Take notice of the impact of your practices, after monitoring and assessing company progress. Self-analysis is a key part of this process. Ensure that a corrective strategy does not cause or result in unfairness.

DISCUSSION Communicate and reinforce the message that diversity is a business asset and a key element of business success in a national and global market.

INCLUSION Bring everyone into this process, including White males. Help them understand that EEO initiatives are good for the company and, thus, good for everyone in the company. Include them in the analysis, planning, and implementation.

DEDICATION Stay persistent in your quest. Long term gains from these practices may cost in the short term. Invest the needed human and capital resources.

Based on the review of the state DOT and transit files, as well as a review of the available literature, the research team identified agencies and companies that appear to implement best practices in their equal employment opportunity efforts.

Public Sector

The state DOTs and transit agencies that exhibited the best practices were those agencies that met the four-pronged framework of compliance, consistency, comprehensiveness, and confidence. These agencies were compliant in that they submitted an EEO-4 and/or FHWA-1392 form, as required by law; collected data consistent with the EEO categories; developed a comprehensive affirmative action plan, including a detailed utilization and availability analysis, as well as an analysis of the application flow; and were able to exhibit confidence in their data due to the implementation of a continuous review and internal monitoring system. Although many of the agencies are doing a good job, the Virginia Department of Transportation was one of the agencies that satisfied the four Cs.

Virginia DOT

The Virginia Department of Transportation met the four-pronged framework of compliance, consistency, comprehensiveness, and confidence. This agency's affirmative action plan showed a sincere commitment to diversity, an understanding of how to create a diverse workforce, and the importance of making sure the entire organization is held accountable for achieving diversity.

The DOT commissioner evidenced his commitment to diversity by stating

> I am committed to the goal of affirmative action, and expect for each manager, supervisor and employee to embrace the goal. The responsibility for affirmative action will be expected and shared by all management personnel. You will be held accountable for your actions in the area and will be evaluated on carrying out these responsibilities.

Achieving diversity goals is not just the responsibility of those individuals or departments specifically charged with affirmative action duties, rather the Commissioner himself also takes responsibility for achieving these goals:

> The success of any organization's programs ultimately rests with the head of the organization. As head of the Virginia Department of Transportation, the Commissioner is charged with responsibility and authority for ensuring that VDOT is a place where employees and applicants for employment can participate in VDOT's employment processes and programs without regard to personal characteristics. And where employees are valued for their professional contributions and the diversity of experience and thought they bring to the workplace. The Commissioner has vested and shares this authority and responsibility with the Civil Rights Division Administrator who is designated as the chief Affirmative Action Officer for VDOT.

The Virginia DOT has several programs in place designed to assist the agency in recruiting minority talent:

- Engineer Development Program—This 24-month development program provides valuable experience and hands-on training in engineering. Graduates play a vital role in roadway design and construction, while enabling participants to choose a career path that focuses on a specific goal. Upon completion of the program, participants are eligible for a highly responsible position in field management at a VDOT residency or district office, where they will be involved in construction, project, or maintenance administration of a multi-county area.
- Engineering Scholarship Program—A scholarship stipend of $7,000 per year ($3,500 each semester) is available to rising sophomores, juniors, and seniors. Summer employment under the supervision of a designated mentor at VDOT begins the summer before the first scholarship award. If qualified, participants may gain full-time employment as an associate engineer at a VDOT location upon graduation.
- Summer Transportation Institute Program—VDOT continues its participation in the Summer Transportation Institute Program hosted by Virginia State University and Hampton University. During this intensive four-week residential program, high school students were introduced to a variety of interdisciplinary careers that contribute to the building and management of highways and bridges.

The agency also has a very good monitoring and evaluation system in place.

- An internal reporting system has been developed to continually audit, monitor, and evaluate programs, which are essential to the success of the affirmative program. This system provides for the establishment of affirmative action plan action items, EEO goals, timetable, and periodic evaluations, which will be monitored by the affirmative action officer.
- Statistics are maintained using the five major racial/gender groups, categorized by EEO-4 occupational categories. Reports are regularly provided to the affirmative action officer and the district civil rights managers. These reports contain agency-wide statistical data for new hires, promotions, terminations, training, and overall employment.

- Status reports are provided throughout the year to the affirmative action officer by the district civil rights managers. The status reports will contain an analysis of the statistical data for the district, results achieved toward established objectives, the identification of particular problems encountered and recommendations for corrective actions needed.
- As a part of the goal setting process, the Affirmative Action Officer will utilize the comparative employment analysis to compare the rate of VDOT's employment of females and minorities within the various EEO-4 categories with the employment of females and minorities in corresponding categories in the labor market area relevant to that work force. In order to develop parity within the workforce, the affirmative action officer will utilize the results of this analysis to establish objectives within the agency with timetables for accomplishment.
- Application of the four-fifths rule is used to determine whether there is evidence of adverse impact.
- VDOT recognizes the fact that affirmative action is a means to an end.
- The applicant tracking system (PaRTS) has been implemented and is being used to monitor the application process from receipt of the application until final selection for each position.
- Data regarding the availability of minorities and females in the civilian work force for the current affirmative action plan was obtained from the United States Census Bureau's 2000 EEO Tabulations, EEO data tools, employment by state and local occupation groups for the state of Virginia. This data gives a benchmark of the civilians that are considered to be employable by the Bureau by position. This data was compared to current VDOT employment data by occupational groups, gender and race for the period of July 1, 2003.

One of the reasons why the Virginia DOT seems to have such an effective EEO program could be related to the fact that it has over 10 staff members in the Civil Rights Division. Other agencies likely have a smaller staff.

Canada

Since many researchers have concluded that it is not necessary for an organization to limit its comparison group to

Ohio DOT

Templates for EEO Reporting (adapted from the Ohio Department of Transportation)

Utilization Analysis

Race/Gender (ie. White Females) Job Category	Census %White Females (Census)	Census 80% of Available (Census)	DOT %White Females in DOT	DOT # of White Females (at end of FY)	DOT Total Employees in Occ. Group	Results Underutilization?	Results Distance from Parity (# of Minorities)
Officials and Managers							
Professionals							
Technicians							
Protective Services							
Administrative Support							
Skilled Craft							
Service Maintenance							

New Hire Analysis

Job Category	Non-Minority # Non-Minority Hired	Non-Minority # of Non-Minority Applicants	Non-Minority Non-minority Selection Rate	Minority # of Black females hire	Minority # of Black female applicants	Minority Black female selection rate	Result Adverse Impact?
Officials and Managers							
Professionals							
Technicians							
Protective Services							
Administrative Support							
Skilled Craft							
Service Maintenance							

an organization in the same industry, it is appropriate to not only review best practices in other industries, but also other countries. Canada prepared a very comprehensive report, *Employment Equity in the Federal Public Service 2003–2004* (Public Service Human Resources Management Agency of Canada 2005), which provides a very thorough analysis of the country's availability and utilization of women and minorities. The first chapter of the report addresses where the country is today by providing a statistical overview of the status of women and minorities. It also provides information on the country's progress toward achieving employment equity. It includes the results of an availability analysis for women, aboriginals, visible minorities, and people with disabilities overall and then broken down by hiring and promotion for the period 1988 through 2004 (Public Service Human Resources Management Agency of Canada 2005). Since the report provides an analysis for several years, it allows them to track their progress toward achieving their employment goals.

The benchmarking process is discussed in the report. The report specifically addresses benchmark setting and achievement, accountability, and cultural change. In the report, benchmarks are defined as "targets" that "measure progress toward goals that an organization has set for itself" (Public Service Human Resources Management Agency of Canada 2005). The report acknowledges that benchmarking cannot take place in a vacuum and must "take into account the realities of an organization's operations." It also recognizes that the public sector must address issues that the private sector might not have to address such as merit and civil service issues. Nevertheless, the report indicates that benchmarks should "complement the concept of merit by ensuring that the public service workforce is qualified and representative, reflecting the diversity of Canadian society and the pools from which employees are drawn" (Public Service Human Resources Management Agency of Canada 2005).

The Canadian government ties diversity goals to performance evaluations. According to the Public Service Human Resources Management Agency of Canada (2005), one of the objectives for the year is, "integrating employment equity measures into management accountability frameworks, human resources and business plans, and ensuring that employment equity is an integral part of human resources modernization." In Canada, they also have internal monitoring. One agency monitors their results "twice yearly with analysis of key indicators such as EE representation at the sector and branch level, the number of staffing actions taken, and eligibility for retirement (Public Service Human Resources Management Agency of Canada 2005). In addition to the internal monitoring process, the Canadian Human Rights Commission audits departments and agencies for compliance with the Employment Equity Act, which is similar to the United States' Civil Rights Act.

The Task Force on the Participation of Visible Minorities in the Federal Public Service provided an action plan for increasing the participation of minorities. The action plan suggested that the following steps be taken:

- Set 1 in 5 benchmarks for visible minority participation in Public Service—wide staffing actions (i.e., recruitment, acting appointments, promotion, and development opportunities at executive levels).
- Create support tools to help departments and managers achieve the benchmarks.
- Change the corporate culture in the Public Service to make it welcoming of diversity.
- Develop mechanisms to strengthen existing implementation and accountability frameworks.
- Seek external advice and independent review of implementation.
- Provide financial resources to support implementation.

Holding managers accountable for results is considered a key component for being able to achieve the diversity benchmarks. According to the report, holding managers accountable for diversity benchmarks will require a change in culture. In order to hold middle managers accountable, middle managers are provided with tools that

- Demonstrate the commitment of senior management;
- Debunk myths regarding the hiring of visible minority employees;
- Recognize, share and reward good practices in visible minority recruitment; and
- Explain the sanctions that managers who do not meet their hiring obligations will face.

Another key factor in helping departments achieve diversity goals is funding. "The Treasury Board Ministers approved up to $30 million in funds for the Employment Equity: Embracing Change Support Fund during the first three years. This initial funding was intended to develop infrastructure and support both central agency and departmental initiatives" (Public Service Human Resources Management Agency of Canada 2005).

Department of Interior

The research team identified the Department of Interior in the discussion of best practices, not because it is a good example of an agency that has a diverse workforce and fully utilizes women and minorities, but because it has implemented a good process for trying to achieve the goal of having a diverse workforce and making sure women and minorities are fully utilized within the agency's workforce.

The Department of Interior has shown a commitment to diversifying its workforce. It developed a presentation that includes information about what successful agencies have in common with regard to equal employment opportunity programs. According to the presentation, successful agencies

- Communicate importance from the top;
- Include an EEO performance element in the performance standards of managers and supervisors;
- Create cross-functional teams to work on various problems/barriers;
- Meet regularly with EEO officials and agency leadership to relay progress;
- Meet regularly with EEO officials and counterparts from agencies of a similar size to share ideas and resources;
- Provide extensive EEO training to all new employees; and
- Review EEO policy and EEO performance elements within one month of an individual gaining supervisory status.[1]

In addition to developing this presentation of best practices, the Department of Interior also developed a strategic plan that specifically addresses diversity. The plan, *Strategic Plan for Achieving and Maintaining a Highly Skilled and Diverse Workforce FY 2005–2009*, has five major focus areas:

- Educate managers, supervisors, and employees regarding the importance of a highly skilled and diverse workforce.
- Step up recruitment efforts for a diverse workforce.
- Improve retention of a diverse workforce.
- Have zero tolerance for discrimination, harassment, and retaliation.
- Ensure accountability for improving diversity. (U.S. Department of Interior 2005)

The Department plans to use statistics to measure the Department's success in achieving a diverse workforce:

> Success in achieving this will be measured by statistical analysis of the Bureaus' and Offices' (1) applicant flow data by race, national origin, disability, and sex for permanent and temporary employment; (2) increased participation rates by race, national origin, disability, and sex in mission critical occupations and leadership ranks, in comparison with the relevant Civilian Labor Force (RCLF)1; and (3) diversity projections identified in Bureau/ Office workforce plans. (U.S. Department of Interior 2005, p. 16)

---

[1]The Best of the FY 2004 MD-715 Reports

The Department developed a detailed list of action steps, established corresponding performance measures, and identified the officials responsible for achieving each step. A few of the action steps and performance measures are provided below:

Private Sector

IBM

IBM (International Business Machines Corporation) is listed in the EEOC's *Best Practices of Private Sector Employers* (EEOC 1997*)*. It is included in this list because it has exhibited a commitment to diversity for many years. IBM is considered a leader in diversity because:

> It demonstrated its commitment to equal employment opportunities before Title VII was passed. In 1962, two years prior to the enactment of Title VII, IBM joined "the federal government's "Plans for Progress"—a voluntary effort to aggressively promote and implement equal employment opportunity.

According to the EEOC report:

- In 1962, "IBM's minority population totaled 1,250, or 1.5% of its U.S. workforce. By the end of 1996, minorities had increased to more than 22,000 regular employees, or 19.4%."
- IBM has not only seen an increase in the number of minority employees, but it has also seen an increase in the number of women. Between 1962 and 1996, "the number of women regular employees grew to over 33,400 or 29.4%. More than 4,100 women and more than 2,200 minority employees held management positions at the end of 1996; and of these, more than 2,400 were in senior management."

Action	Performance Measure	Responsible Officials
Increase workforce participation of women, minorities, and people with disabilities.	Percent age of diversity increased in the applicant pool of people applying for employment across the Department	Bureau Managers and Supervisors
Train managers and supervisors in use of available personnel tools, authorities, regulations, and procedures.	Percentage of managers and supervisors trained on personnel tools, authorities, regulations and procedures	Bureau Managers, Supervisors and HR Officials
Develop and use targeted recruitment plans to expand pool of qualified applicants.		Bureau Managers and Supervisors
Maintain a tracking system for applicant flow data by race, national origin, sex, disability, and related disposition.		Bureau HR and EEO Officials
Evaluate statistical analyses of permanent and temporary workforce participation rates by grade level and race, national origin, sex, and disability; and rates of selection for promotions, training opportunities and performance incentives.	Percentage of improvement in the retention of women, minorities, and people with disabilities	Bureau Manages and Supervisors

- "Women were first placed in professional positions in 1936, and the first woman vice president was named in 1943.
- The first Black sales representative was hired in 1946, and a Black engineering manager was named in 1956.
- IBM's first written statement of equal opportunity, which reinforced its commitment to nondiscriminatory hiring practices, was published in 1953, more than a decade before the landmark Civil Rights Act of 1964."
- IBM says that it sets goals by job groups, and the goals are based on the populations in the feeder groups—those jobs from which the company typically recruits to fill particular positions.
- The company indicates that goals are not quotas. In hiring and promoting, goals are flexible and require good faith efforts on the part of IBM managers.

APPENDIX F

Acronyms and Abbreviations

EEO—equal employment opportunity
EEOC—Equal Employment Opportunity Commission
FHWA—Federal Highway Administration
FTA—Federal Transit Administration
OFCCP—Office of Federal Contract Compliance
SDOT—state department of transportation
TRB—Transportation Research Board
USDOT—U.S. Department of Transportation